Jacked

Also by Nomi Prins

Other People's Money: The Corporate Mugging of America

Jacked

How "Conservatives" Are Picking Your Pocket

(*WHETHER YOU VOTED FOR THEM OR NOT*)

NOMI PRINS

P³

PoliPointPress

Jacked: How "Conservatives" Are Picking Your Pocket - Whether You Voted for Them or Not by Nomi Prins

This edition published in 2006 in the United States of America by PoliPointPress, P.O. Box 3008, Sausalito, CA 94966
www.p3books.com

Production management: Michael Bass Associates
Book design: Linda M. Robertson, LMR Designs
Cover design: Robin Awes

Library of Congress Cataloging-In-Publication Data

Prins, Nomi
Jacked: How "Conservatives" Are Picking Your Pocket - Whether You Voted for Them or Not I Nomi Prins

ISBN: 0-9760621-8-6

Library of Congress Control Number: 2006902590

Printed in the United States of America
June 2006

Published by:
PoliPointPress, LLC
P.O. Box 3008
Sausalito, CA 94966-3008
(415) 339-4100
www.p3books.com

Distributed by Publishers Group West

To my father,

who moved to Mexico because Bush was re-elected.

Contents

Introduction

Once upon a time, families talked about politics over dinner, hit TV shows like *M*A*S*H* openly questioned war, and people didn't fall in love over the Internet. In the early 1980s, Bruce Springsteen's *Born in the USA* was the working person's anthem, and it was cool; at the 2005 Grammy awards, Green Day's timely album, *American Idiot*, got six nominations. Somewhere along the way, we changed. Pride and cynicism switched positions—particularly when it came to politics.

It's not that politics became less important; it's that more Americans checked out of the conversation. That's one reason for the declining voter turnout over the past couple of decades, and the fact that many people tend not to trust either of the major parties.[1] If you can't connect to your leaders or feel they "get" you, it's only natural to disconnect from what they're saying. Maybe that's why more people recognize the judges on *American Idol* than the judges on the Supreme Court. It's easier to relate to would-be singers with dreams than to guys in robes—or pundits in suits, for that matter. Plus, it takes time to follow these issues as you're battling traffic, working a job you hate to pay off the school loans that got you there, or stretching your Social Security checks.

But politics still touches our everyday lives in so many different ways. So taking the nature of our frantic lives into account, I've tried to talk about American politics by starting with something we can all relate to—our wallets. Wallets are roadmaps of our daily realities: they hold photos of the people we love, chunks of our identity, and plastic cards that evoke our financial worries. The cards inside your wallet tell a story. They also tell the tale of the government's impact on you.

This book traces those impacts. The driver's license chapter connects the price you pay at the gas pump to our country's policies on energy and Iraq. The health insurance chapter talks about Medicare, Medicaid, and those ridiculous insurance premiums we all hate. The credit card chapter examines personal debt, credit card company profits, and the skyrocketing national debt. The student identification chapter looks at mounting educational expenses and reduced governmental support for what is supposed to be the country's most valuable asset—its brains. And so on. I've tried to untangle the web our government weaves around and through our frantic lives. So *Jacked* is for anyone who struggles to pay bills, needs health care, is looking for a job, or feels their company is not keeping its promises to them. It's for anyone who has questioned the government's role in it all.

Soon after the idea for this book first hit me, I realized I didn't want to write it from a desk in New York City or Washington, DC. I once worked in a world (called Wall Street) that disregards pretty much *everyone* outside of its own sphere. This isn't exactly the greatest way to understand what's really going on in our country. So I traveled the United States by plane, train, automobile, and ferry. I went through the rubble of Hurricane Katrina in places CNN hadn't lingered, toured subsidized housing blocks for the elderly who can barely stretch the Social Security they get, and sat with Latino students determined to get their educations.

As a result, I got an education, too. Crisscrossing thirty states over four months, I interviewed nearly one thousand people and met many more. They had an astounding diversity of backgrounds and beliefs, but one thing in common. A wallet. (Well, some had money clips or rubber bands or purses, but you get the idea.) They might not all have had the same amount of money, but they sure had plenty of cards: from credit cards to organ donor cards, from library cards to Candy's Car Wash ("Buy 10 get 1 free"). I talked to people in cities and tiny rural towns in the middle of nowhere; in red and blue states; to the old and the young; to those educated by college or by life; to the poor and the well off. I followed Bush's path through the Gulf Coast, spent time at UAW headquarters in Detroit, spoke with authors in Alabama, tile contractors in northern Washington, jazz musicians in New Orleans, and military officers in California. Over lots of coffee and beer and pie, with tour guides and health-care workers, single parents and struggling seniors, the politically active and those who are too busy worrying about other things, I learned more about this amazing country than I thought possible.

One of the things I learned is that no matter what their conditions, Americans are inspiring. The people I met help keep this country strong. They give it labor and breath. When you peel away their surface differences, they have similar dreams, too, even if our laws, political priorities, and social conditions make some of these dreams harder to achieve than others. The more I listened, the angrier I got about recent decisions made in Washington; the more I felt that our government is letting us down. Nowhere did I feel this more than in Waveland, Mississippi.

JUST A WAVE IN WAVELAND

In the midst of my travels, I arrived at Waveland, Mississippi, the last Gulf Coast town before the Louisiana border, 17 feet above sea level. It used to have 7,000 inhabitants. That was before it caught Hurricane Katrina's eye and was trounced by a 32-foot water surge. When I visited there in mid-January 2006, its population was 1,000. Right before the exit off Interstate 10, there's a smaller town called Diamond Head. I stopped at a Burger King there, for the millionth Diet Coke of my cross-country trip. Its notice board read: *Almost back to normal and getting better.*

But before you reach the shoreline, the damage becomes more and more apparent. Pieces of signs line the highway where the wind blew them months before. Animal carcasses litter the shoulder, lying dead for days, because debris gets take-away priority. Scrawled on a tiny olive-green deserted home off Route 603 are the words "The South will rise again." Heading farther west on Route 90, that's hard to believe. That's when it hits you. It's like *War of the Worlds* after the scary aliens zap your home. But they don't die in the end; the humans don't return victoriously to reclaim their street. In the heart of Waveland, there is simply nothing left. Silence has won the battle.

There are no houses, no frames, no bedrock—just pieces of walls, slivers of wood, shards of glass, wheels of toy trucks, bits of refrigerators, all mixed with fallen trees stripped bare of leaves by wind and water. Street after street after street. It's the kind of destruction that numbs you, stops you cold. I couldn't keep the tears back or my throat clear. And there, in the land of the new nowhere, I spotted an old man in overalls standing beside his battered navy blue Ford pickup, wiping his forehead.

I brought my car to a stop at what would have been two house lengths away from him, if there were any houses left. Hands on hips, he seemed to be taking a break. I couldn't think of a good way to start the conversation, so I just blurted out,

"Hi, do you have a minute—to chat?"

He said sweetly,

"Sure, I've got lots of time. This stuff is pretty slow-going."

Like he has done every day since the storm, Gordon Coleman is sorting through the wreckage that was his home. Haggard and stooped, he prides himself on the new foundation he's created, the only plot of land on his street showing any signs of a comeback. He's managed to clear enough to rebuild the base. An old wheelbarrow stands on the other side of his truck. He uses it as part of his daily one-man removal program. There is a smile in Gordon's crinkled gray eyes. The dirt caked under his fingernails is dirt of determination. He shrugs his shoulders and says,

"You just gotta go on."

Two days earlier, President Bush drove by this town en route to New Orleans. He had given a speech at a boys school in nearby Bay St. Louis, praising the progress made in the region. Whatever planet that was on. A group of Wavelanders were eager to meet him, and had made posters welcoming him and eager to help. But Bush didn't stop in their town—all they got, as they put it, was a "wave in Waveland."

A few weeks later, Bush didn't even mention Mississippi in his 2006 State of the Union address. He barely discussed the nation's largest natural disaster at all. A month after that, Katrina victims—many of whom lost their homes and hadn't received insurance or government claim money—were being kicked out of their temporary accommodations.[2] While all of this was happening, Bush paid lip service to the progress being made in the area and spilled more words and spent more money on the Middle East.

Two months later, I returned to Gordon Coleman's lot on Hillcrest Road in Waveland. It was a beautiful sunny April afternoon, dry and clear. The Ford was parked at the back of his property. It looked like it hadn't been driven for a while. The wheelbarrow was gone. So were signs of Gordon. I asked one lone woman working on her yard nearer the shore if she knew of his whereabouts—she shook her head "no," looking at me as if I was crazy.

The damage our government is doing is not reserved just for situations as dramatic as Katrina; Bush's same brand of "disconnect" can be seen in many of his decisions about our wallets and what they are to us.

WHAT DOES YOUR WALLET BUY?

The quick answer is—less than it used to. But you already know that. The real income of the typical American household has fallen five years in a row, despite the fact that the economy expanded during three of those years. Over the same period, we Americans became more productive; in fact, our output per hour went up 15 percent.[3] That means that we're working our butts off with less to show for it. Instead of requiring companies to pay higher minimum wages, or increase—rather than decrease—benefits, or pay taxes they legally owe, our government has consistently focused its attention elsewhere. Although the job market expanded in 2004, it was not enough to absorb the labor market slack left over after the longest jobless recovery on record.[4] Translation: corporations were profitable, but didn't use the money they made to pay the average employee more, hire more American workers, or increase benefits.

Your driver's license entitled you to pay twice as much per gallon of gas in 2006 as in 2000. If you fast forward through 2006, Hurricane Katrina will probably be blamed for those high gas prices. But prices had already risen 60 percent since the Iraq war, and only rose an additional 10 percent following Katrina. Even before Katrina hit, while relaxing on his Texas ranch Bush signed the latest energy bill into law, giving energy companies billions of dollars of fresh tax breaks.[5]

Then there's your credit card and the larger issue of debt. In 2004, 1.6 million Americans filed for personal bankruptcy protection, a fivefold increase from 1980.[6] In February 2005, the Senate passed the biggest reform of bankruptcy in a quarter of a century. President Bush signed it into law in April 2005.[7] This made it harder for us to declare personal bankruptcy, but kept it just as easy for corporations. And who crafted the bill? That's right. Credit card companies.

There's your debit/ATM card. If you think your money is not stretching as far as it used to, you're not imagining things. Banks spend hours determining how to use your relationship with them to suck money from you. Take fees: there's no reason banks have to charge people to access their own money. And yet what happens if you can't maintain a minimum balance? You pay a fee. Don't do direct deposit because you need the cash from your paycheck immediately? Pay a fee.

Take a look at your health insurance card—if you have one. Almost 46 million Americans (or 15.7 percent of the population) don't, including 8.4 million children.[8] That number has increased every year since President Bush took office. Besides those with no insurance, there are millions more with limited coverage. About four million Americans lost employment-based health insurance during George W. Bush's first term alone.[9]

Then there's your Social Security card. If it's anything like mine, it's frayed around the edges from having been stuck behind the other cards. So is the system it represents. Social Security taxes are collected on earnings up to $90,000. Unfortunately, 94 percent of the country doesn't make that much, and people who make million dollar salaries pass that mark by mid-January. The Bush Republicans aren't trying to even that out—quite the opposite. Their push to privatize Social Security would mean even less financial security for those who most need it. And the idea of private accounts so people can make their own financial decisions? I used to be a banker, but even I don't have the time to analyze the stock market. Nor the trust that it won't tank when I retire.

WHERE'S THE AMERICAN DREAM?

It wasn't always this unequal. Corporations used to pay more to the government, and CEOs weren't paid if they screwed things up. At the end of World War II, corporations paid half the cost of the federal government. Guess what that percentage is now: about 7 percent. Meanwhile, 60 percent of corporations didn't pay *any* federal taxes at all, even during their best years.[10]

If you were middle class and white, a college education used to be pretty much a given. Now it's becoming the realm of the upper class. Most college graduates earn more than nongraduates, yet the college experience keeps getting more expensive. The average cost of tuition and fees at four-year colleges went up 11 percent in 2004. Average student loan debt almost doubled in the last 10 years. Instead of broadening opportunities for education, and thus our standing in the world, at the end of 2005 the House approved the biggest cut to higher education funding ever. The Senate followed suit in February 2006.[11] With rising college costs, gaps in enrollment by income and race are larger than they were three decades ago. Students from lower-income and minority families are far less likely to enroll in college and finish four-year degrees.[12]

One in four Americans owes more than he or she can afford in debt. Seven out of 10 middle-class Americans live paycheck to paycheck. The situation is worse if you're black or Hispanic. Wages are declining, and so are lifestyles. Overall, almost a third of working families have incomes below the basic family budget levels that are estimated annually by our government, and 9.4 percent live below poverty levels. And what's the worst city in the country for making ends meet? It's Washington, DC. Our nation's capitol. The backyard of the President (when he's not golfing) and Congress. Almost half of its inhabitants have family incomes below family budget levels.[13]

After President Bush's abysmal response to Hurricane Katrina, 60 percent of Americans polled said he didn't share their priorities for the country, a 10-point drop from his fall 2004 re-election levels. Over half disapproved of his overall performance. Half of the public felt the economy was deteriorating.[14] Fortunately, elections are coming up, giving us an opportunity to at least address our congressional state and local politicians. But midterm elections never draw much attention. Only 38 percent of the population voted in the 2002 midterm election, compared to half in the 2000 and 2004 presidential elections.[15] We've got to change that.

There are lots of laws and even more money stacked against the average American. It seems overwhelming when you think about it. That's why we need to break it down. Each of us needs to decide what matters most, and then find out what the government is really doing about it, or what it should be doing.

SO WHAT GETS TO YOU?

There are some things you can't make yourself do no matter how many opportunities you get. You can't be friendly to a telemarketer. You can't be patient while the cable company puts you on perma-hold. You can't calmly give the last four digits of your Social Security number to the twelfth person in a row when all you want is the answer to a simple billing question from your electric company. I'm with you on all of this.

Other events can be even more aggravating. The one that really got me was President Bush's fourth visit and zillionth photo-op in New Orleans following Katrina. Switching on my TV set to watch him ooze concern for people and a city he had ignored for years made me want to chuck the unit out my window. This is a man who has spent over $320 billion dollars (and counting) waging an unsubstantiated, unending war in Iraq, which has killed over 2,500 of our soldiers, increased the defense budget, and provided defense contractors their most profitable years ever.[16] All under the guise of strengthening the Department of Homeland Security that he created to, well, secure the homeland. By the time Bush decided to take *some* responsibility for Homeland Security's complete incompetence in dealing with Katrina, over 1,000 bodies had been discovered, drowned and dehydrated.

Under our president's leadership, Americans are working harder and taking home less. An additional 22 million of us live in poverty or below basic family budget levels since he took office. Fewer can afford college. Fewer have health insurance. Fewer will have financial security when they retire. Not because the federal government can't help, but because the majority party chooses not to. If they followed policies that promoted our "general welfare" as the Constitution states, we'd not only be richer individually, but stronger as a nation.

In polls taken after the disaster, the majority of Americans said they would roll back tax cuts to help Katrina victims, something that didn't occur to our president. His choices puff company coffers while draining the wallets of ordinary citizens. It's depressing. It's enough to make you feel too helpless to stop it. You're too busy stretching your paycheck, feeding your kids, and caring for your parents. So take a deep breath, open your wallet, and read about what people just like you all over the country are going through.

This book will make you aware of what you're not getting from your government, why you're not getting it, what you're entitled to, and how to get it. It will also show you that you're not alone. If we do this right, politicians in Washington will become more concerned about the people they represent. That's what real America should be. Real people, real wallets, real soul, real ideas—and that's what you'll find in the following chapters.

DMV CALIFORNIA DMV

DRIVER LICENSE
B55555555

CLASS: C

EXPIRES 01-26-08

Jane Q. Public
555 Anystreet
Anytown USA 55555

EYES :BRN
DOB:01-26-79

Sex: F Hair: Black
Ht: 5-07 WT: 125

Jane Q. Public
05/07/2003 548 32 FD/08

1

Your Driver's License, Oil, and Gas Prices

The morning rain is torrential. It's like nature can't give New Orleans a break. At my French Quarter hotel on St. Ann Street, there is a mix of displaced families, journalists, and camera crews. There don't seem to be any tourists.

No matter what color they are, the few people roaming the streets are embarrassed by Mayor Ray Nagin's statements about rebuilding New Orleans as a chocolate city. They point out that the city has other problems right now. More of that spirit is displayed on T-shirts hanging along Bourbon Street gift shops:

Katrina—You Bitch!

New Orleans: Proud to Swim Home

Make Levees, Not War

I decide to buy my favorite one:

FEMA—The New Four Letter Word

It's my contribution to the local economy.

The tourist information center is empty except for two older women—Shirley and Eleanor—who work there part time. Eleanor suggests I call Ozzie LaPorte to take me around the city. She whispers,

"He's a very handsome man."

Ten minutes later, Ozzie picks me up in his white tour van off Jackson Square. At 54, he comes from five generations of New Orleanders.

"I got purple, green, and gold blood in my veins—the Mardi Gras colors. Red beans and rice, too," he says.

His laughter is infectious. After working for 10 years as a driver and guide with Celebration Tours, he bought the company in September 2004. Ozzie relies on two things to make a living, both of which involve driving—taking tourists around and reasonable fuel costs.

Ozzie's plans for his new company haven't quite panned out. The price of gas, which has doubled since Bush took office, but really climbed after his second inauguration, didn't help. At $1.50 per gallon before the war in Iraq, gas prices were at $1.80 four months after Ozzie became his own boss and steadily rose throughout 2005. They shot to $3.07 per gallon after Katrina.[1] It was around that period that Ozzie geared up to celebrate his first anniversary.

"Great timing—huh?" he shrugs.

Before the hurricane, his city tour never ventured any-where near the Lower Ninth Ward.

"We'd talk about the canals," he says proudly. "Venice has 68 miles—we have 'em beat with 170 miles of canals. Did you know that?"

I didn't. Now, the few people that use his services want to see the canals that broke and the neighborhoods that were destroyed. So he felt obliged to rename the tour, and now calls it "the Disaster Tour." He's able to get only to the least affected areas outside the decimated Ninth Ward with his vans, out of a combination of respect and the local government's desire to keep the devastation under wraps.

On Harrison Avenue, closer to the lakefront, you begin to see water marks lining the sides of houses. These stains are four to five feet above the ground. Turning onto St. Bernard Avenue, a predominately middle-class white and upper-class black neighborhood, homes are marked with big spray-painted Xs. These are SOS signs for the Federal Emergency Management Agency (FEMA). There is still no electricity here. A few FEMA trailers stand in front of houses where people are doing clean-up work while it's still daylight. Many more of these trailers have been standing vacant in parking lots for months, not yet dispatched to house some of the desperate and waiting families. So—not surprising that FEMA is "The New Four Letter Word."

"Four of my vans were stolen out of six after the hurricane," says Ozzie. "One showed up in an armed robbery in Houston three months after Katrina."

Once Katrina hit in late August, gas prices jumped sharply—on fears, said Wall Street analysts, that too much damage was incurred by oil refineries on the coastline. In some states, prices jumped over a dollar a gallon as crude oil, which makes up about half the price of a gallon of gas, soared to an all-time high of $70 a barrel.

Simultaneously, Wall Street energy traders were already dreaming up ways to spend their record year-end bonuses. Certainly better days for them than when the average price of crude was only $28.50 a barrel in 2003—before Iraq—or $37 in 2004. War and wind do wonders for seven-figure takes. They had their own record year as a result.

Meanwhile, Ozzie returned from evacuation in Little Rock, Arkansas, to his broken city and lost business.

"You did get some FEMA money," he says. "I got $2,000, some people got $4,300. It doesn't cover much. I had to start putting gas on my credit card."

Five months after Katrina, they're still uncovering dead bodies in the Ninth Ward and since the city won't let tour vans in the area, Ozzie and I drive my Toyota rental into St. Bernard Parish and the Lower Ninth. There's wreckage everywhere: one house rests on a pickup truck, the sidewalks are littered with soggy old mattresses, trash, pieces of picture frames still attached to forever-damp bits of smiling families.

"That's why the opened bars are doing well—people need to vent—too much of this, day in and day out, will drive you crazy, anyone crazy."

In 2004, the seven largest American oil companies earned $51 billion. For 2005, their take rose to $70 billion. Oil companies made an extra $25 billion in profits between July and September because of rising gas prices and the effects of Hurricanes Katrina and Rita.

OIL CAPITAL OF AMERICA

Houston, Texas, is both the place where Ozzie's vans wound up as accessories in a felony robbery and the oil capital of the United States. At his home, in a secluded area of mini-communities each indistinguishable from the next (after I've already gotten lost several times trying to find the right one), I meet with Steve Miller. He looks like a stern Paul Newman with clear blue eyes and a chiseled face. After graduating from Texas Tech with a business degree, Steve entered the oil service business.

"All my adult life, I worked in pipe, horizontal and vertical,"

says Steve, a vice president of sales and marketing for a pipe firm.[2] He's wearing a blue and white cap, blue jeans, black flip-flops and a Ralph Lauren shirt checkered with the colors of the American flag. His home is lovely, complete with a carefully crafted pool and nearby golf greens. He drives about 30,000 miles a year for work, slightly more than the national average. For a number of reasons, he doesn't think gas prices will come down any time soon, if ever.

> *"Not," says Steve, "unless there's a recession and people stop buying. In Texas, that's attributable to different factors. First, there's no real mass transit. Second, it's part of the old west mentality—I got my horse, I'm gonna ride it.* [Of course, now that horse is a gas-guzzling beast.] *And third, even if gas goes to $5 a gallon, people in Texas will still drive."*

Before Katrina, crude oil prices were at a then-record high of $66 per barrel. The Senate had just approved a bill to revamp energy policy. It encouraged more efficient use of energy, development of renewable fuels like ethanol, and declared that 10 percent of utility-produced electricity be generated by renewable sources like wind, solar, and nuclear plants by the year 2020.[3]

The bill passed by a vote of 85 to 12, after two weeks of debate on how best to deal with the soaring oil and gas prices. The decision was—do nothing to cap them. Still, the landslide passage of this bill was a tepid indication that the folks in Washington at least occasionally acknowledged the dire situation of energy consumption. (In a telling irony, however, soon thereafter the Department of Energy announced it would lay off 40 members from its renewable energy laboratory staff, due to a 15 percent decrease in their funding.[4]) And even as the Senate seemed to be advocating alternative solutions to our reliance on big oil, their bill still managed to provide a hefty perk for these same companies—an additional $16 billion of oil company tax breaks over the next 10 years. This doubled the amount requested by an earlier House version of the same bill.

A strong oil lobby was largely responsible for this change, after they stressed that the business has its ups and downs and needs government support. Unfortunately, most of us are far removed from these behind-the-scenes maneuvers, despite their huge impact on our lives. And driving remains so basic to so many of us that Steve thinks Americans will keep paying at the pump no matter what the price.

"Americans have to get adjusted to higher gas prices, like Europeans did years ago."

The oil business has been through volatile times before. It was slow after the 1973 oil embargo, but eventually rebounded. By 1981, the industry had 4,500 rigs drilling for oil in the 48 states. Then, it went south again. By April 1999 there were only 488 rigs.

"Now," says Steve, "we're back to 1,500 and think we're doing great. If Detroit had taken the hit that the oil drilling business did, it'd have been out of business years ago."

Thanks to the cozy relationship between big oil and government, the industry will continue to thrive. Particularly helpful for corporate interests, and unhelpful for middle-class drivers, is instability in major oil areas in the Middle East.

But all in all, Steve is pretty upbeat about the financial state of America.

"I'm amazed at the resilience of the economy," he says. "It floors me—through the dot com spiral, 9/11, price of crude, shape of airlines and automobile industry, hurricanes. If you'd asked me eight years ago, I'd have said, buy gold coins and hide them in the backyard, it'd be Armageddon."

His son Drew, who has stopped by his parents' house for homemade 30th birthday cookies, doesn't quite share his Dad's optimism.

"The economy isn't as good as it was when Clinton was in office," he says,

his blue–green eyes flashing. Drew works for the third-largest new home construction company in the country.

"I'm doing okay personally," he admits, adjusting his red baseball cap, "because house building is still a growing area, but it could go down the tubes any day, week or year now. I'm worried about the person in office and his policies, because he's an idiot."

He sits down at the patio table and leans back in his chair.

"I'm embarrassed he got reelected and that I live in a red state."

He lowers his voice and looks over his shoulder at his father, now in the kitchen, then turns his head back towards me and says, almost in a whisper:

"I know my father feels differently about this."

Drew's girlfriend, Alicia Brittain, is a 30-year-old single mom, reed-thin with ginger-red hair. She looks 20. Divorced with two kids—an 11-year-old boy, Aaron, and 6-year-old girl, Cameron—her ex pays child support. Otherwise, she couldn't manage. Last fall, she started classes at North Harris Community College. Tuition is affordable, but the $500 a semester for books is steep. She makes too much to qualify for government assistance, but childcare—along with everything else—is expensive, and she lives paycheck to paycheck.

"I used to think 'middle class' meant two cars, two paychecks," she says. "Now I'm not sure where I fall—I think middle and lower middle classes get neglected in this country."

She's not alone in thinking this. As the upper classes amass more and more of the country's wealth, the middle class is being squeezed by, among other things, increases in their basic living costs.

For Alicia and millions of other Americans, there's the double whammy of high transportation and heating costs, even in a state like Texas, with huge highways and where the average winter temperature is 60 degrees.

"When gas goes up, for my car or my electric bill to heat my home, I feel it," says Alicia. "Like this month, my Centrepoint

gas bill was really high—and usually in the winter when gas goes up, electric at least goes down, but this past winter, it was up too. Maybe they should have a system for subsidizing energy costs."

That would be a smart idea.

But there really isn't a system for capping or subsidizing heating costs for the middle class. Energy companies became increasingly less regulated over the past decade. In the mid-1990s, energy companies initially kept prices competitive to reassure customers, but then raised them as they took over more market share in the regions they serviced, effectively giving consumers little choice in their providers.[5] This trend will only continue, thanks to the Republican House Energy Policy Act signed by Bush in August 2005. The bill abolished New Deal–era rules that had protected consumers from being gouged by requiring the government to regulate public utility companies.[6] (And in a separate, but similarly painful move, in February 2006 the Bush administration supported the reduction of a home fuel assistance program for lower income citizens.[7])

BULL'S-EYE FOR OIL COMPANIES AND WALL STREET OIL TRADERS

By late September 2005, oil prices were reported to have "sagged"—to $65 dollars a barrel!—prompting Federal Reserve Chairman Alan Greenspan to praise the economy for weathering the increase in oil prices "reasonably well."[8] Apparently, Alan Greenspan doesn't stop by roadside gas stations to fill up his own tank.

A month later, oil popped back to new highs. The Bush Republicans managed to get an oil refinery bill passed anyway, providing profitable federal subsidies to the oil companies, but again, nothing to the American drivers who rely on this oil for their livelihood.[9] Come November 2005, people didn't feel any better about the gas price pinch. Mounting public pressure prompted the Senate Energy and Commerce committees to summon CEOs from oil company giants Chevron, Conoco Phillips, BP America, Exxon Mobil, and Shell Oil to explain exactly why they were booking record profits off the country's worst hurricane.[10] Remarkably, the oil execs weren't required to testify under oath, like *everyone else* questioned by the Senate. On November 9, 2005, they sat in front of a Senate panel chaired by Senator Ted Stevens (R-Alaska), who rubberstamped their special treatment. He said:

> The question's been raised . . . whether . . . I should administer oaths to these witnesses at today's hearings. . . . These witnesses . . . are aware that making false statements . . . is a violation of federal law, whether or not an oath has been administered. I shall not administer an oath today.

Thanks, Ted. But wait, Ted—they *did* make false statements. Either that or, when asked, they "forgot" where they were during the price gouging in California, when icons of corruption like Enron were extracting exorbitant electricity fees from the wallets of ordinary Californians while plumping up the wallets of their senior execs.

In defense of their enormous oil profits, the exec boys told the Senate that they *needed* that money. They had to invest in refineries and exploration. Extra taxes would be a drag. Ignored was the fact that the rest of America was paying their bonuses. Or also needed that money. Echoing a common refrain, Lee Raymond, chairman of Exxon Mobil, realized that high gas prices "put a strain on Americans' house-hold budgets." He just didn't see why that meant his company should bear the brunt of that strain.[11] In 2005, this man made $42 million and retired with an $81.3 million pension package.[12]

In an oddly nonpartisan move, Senator Charles Grassley, a Republican from Iowa, included a $5 billion "backdoor windfall tax" in a Senate Finance Committee bill passed by the committee in November 2005. Apparently, this was supposed to make up for the $60 billion in tax breaks given to the oil companies in the same bill.

Not that these companies need the help. Oil and gas producers already pay well below the normal federal corporate tax rate of 35 percent. The top companies paid an average of 13.3 percent in federal taxes during the first three years of the Bush administration.[13] And according to the energy bill proposed by the House in April 2005, they will also get $8 billion in tax breaks over the next ten years.

Americans use a quarter of the world's oil. The five companies that testified before the Senate are efficient at what they do. Collectively, they produce more oil per day than Saudi Arabia, even though Saudi Arabia sits on the largest oil reserve in the world. Saudi Arabia may sit on lots of oil, but U.S. companies produce refined oil from crude oil in bigger amounts. Since a third of their production occurs on federally owned land, their production costs are small. It costs Exxon Mobil $20 to produce one barrel of oil, so they make $50 when they turn around and sell it to Americans for 70 bucks. Before Bush took office, U.S. oil companies made about 23 cents for every gallon of gasoline they refined from crude oil. After Hurricane Katrina and two and a half years in Iraq, their profit had quadrupled, and they were making 99 cents on the gallon.[14]

BACK TO NEW ORLEANS AND GAS PRICES

After taking a minor post-Katrina breather, by the end of January 2006 crude oil prices had surged back to $68.35 a barrel, their highest price in four months. In mid-February, I spoke again with my tour guide, Ozzie LaPorte, to see how he was doing on the eve of Mardi Gras.

> *"I'm trying to deal and survive right now. I have three vans ready to work, but I'm barely getting tours,"*

he tells me. Ozzie is doing other things to make ends meet: picking people up at the airport, taking them at night to parties.

> *"It's actually given me a chance to be more creative."*

He decided to rename the Disaster Tour, and now called it "the Recovery Tour."

> *"It's a bit more positive sounding,"*

he says. But he also emphasizes, once again, that

> *"the price of gas is an expense I have to deal with to keep moving."*

I ask him what he thinks of the money that oil executives and Wall Street traders were scooping up in 2005, courtesy of Katrina and some Republican friends in Washington.

> *"Honestly, I don't think about those execs very much," he answers. "I'd get depressed—they obviously have better political connections than I do. They can afford to pay lobbyists to*

make things happen for them. I don't happen to have my own lobbyist."

Before Katrina, when he was running two or three vans, Ozzie used to pay $1,200 a month in fuel costs. His business is stuck in a catch-22 situation. Gas is expensive, but he's also operating fewer tours because of the lack of tourism. He dreams for both to even out: lower fuel prices and more tourists.

The Interior Department's latest budget included another bunch of tax giveaways to oil and natural gas companies, $7 billion over the next five years to pump about $65 billion worth of oil and natural gas from federal territory. Bush, a former oil man like his vice president, told the nation in his 2006 State of the Union address that it was "addicted to oil." He probably meant to say, "*I* am addicted to oil," because the energy sector contributed $50.6 million in donations during the 2004 election cycle, 75 percent of it to Republicans. The very next day, while Bush stressed his commitment to alternative sources of energy like ethanol to fight our collective oil addiction, the Department of Energy announced that, due to a fifteen percent cut in funding, it would lay off 40 members from its renewable energy laboratory staff.[15]

Meanwhile, Ozzie drives on and tries to stay optimistic.

"We'll survive," he says. "It's a marathon, not a sprint. Hopefully, the administration has learned something that could help for the 2006 hurricane season."

Unfortunately, I can't share Ozzie's optimism that Bush and his Republicans will change much without intense pressure. The men and women who control our government don't seem to be very good at either learning or helping. Crude oil at 80 bucks a barrel and gas at four bucks a gallon, anyone? It's gonna happen.

Your Credit Cards and
Our National Debt

When Paramount Pictures was looking for the right location to shoot the remake of *Stepford Wives*, starring Nicole Kidman and Bette Midler, it found Fairfield County, Connecticut. Most of the area is a suburban Mecca; a fifty-five minute train ride from Manhattan, a tax haven for hedge funds, and a picturesque scene of stately homes, manicured lawns, and luxury SUVs. But not everyone in Fairfield County lives this idyllic lifestyle.

Margaret Bustell is a working mom of three, including a newborn. Her husband travels often for his media sales job, and she manages career, family, and dog twenty-five hours a day. The morning after she returned from her three-day hospital stay following a C-section, she was settling in on her living room couch, nursing her son.

Jacked

The phone rings. Twice. And stops. A minute later, it rings again. Her mother, who has been helping out after the birth, picks up the receiver.

"Hello?"

she answers. A pause.

"Yes, it is,"

she says, (the home of Margaret Bustell).

"No, she can't" (come to the phone, because she's breast-feeding her infant).

"I don't know" (when it would be more convenient to call back, because she just gave birth).

It is 9 AM. The previous call from this company was at 9 PM the night before.

Margaret is no slacker. In college, she was the only freshman that color-coded her planner. She paid bills on time and had a credit score in the high 700s, or "very good." But, sometimes you just can't do everything at once. So, while juggling the kids, the pregnancy, and the delivery, she was late on a credit card payment. *One* payment.

"The day it was due," she recalls, "I was going into the hospital. My dining room was a disaster—covered with baby gifts. I wasn't thinking about my bills."

Her payment became a week late.

"The only reason I even realized it was late," she says, "is that a week after it was due, they started harassing me, calling early in the morning, late at night, middle of the day. These people are machines."

She sent the minimum payment and some extra. It wasn't until she got her next statement that she noticed she'd been jacked.

"For people big on communicating when they want something," she notes, simultaneously spooning Gerber's for Henry and giving Tucker a treat, "they went silent. They raised my rate with no notice, immediately. My finance charge got huge— like $140. All of a sudden my purchases were at 27.99 percent, from 10.9 percent."

(That would be 27.99 percent, not 28 percent—after all, they're not complete crooks.)

Two weeks later, they started calling again.

"I was like—I just sent it to you, what do you people want?"

This time they told Margaret that they were after the next month's payment.

"They tried to get me to let them link into my personal checking account so they could pull it directly," she adds.

They also charged her an extra $39 for each of the two months.

"I would like to know," says Margaret, "when they're already charging interest and hiking up my rate—how exactly this whole situation costs them an additional $39 a month."

Jacked

Not only do credit card companies commonly zing customers with a late fee upwards of $30, they also use the late payment as a reason to double or triple annual interest rates. In 2005, credit card issuers made $16 billion in penalty fees alone.[1]

> *"They're running rampant and there's no one looking out for the consumer," says Margaret, wiping Henry's mouth. "They make you feel like a deadbeat. Between payments, I had a C-section, couldn't drive for a month, and was homebound. To say you're exhausted is an understatement—a big feat is being able to accomplish a shower."*

The majority of American households are paying more than the minimum payment required each month by their credit cards. Almost half have been called by a bill collector and have missed or been late on at least one payment per year, the result being a late fee at least once or twice a year.[2] Credit card companies can and will: increase your rate at any time; charge any late fee the market will bear (in other words, that will not piss you off enough to cancel the card and transfer your balance); and increase your annual rate to anything they want.

Six months later, Margaret decided to close her account, because of the high interest rate, and switch her $4,500 balance to another card with a zero percent rate. When she called Chase to inform them, the customer service representative got all emotional on her. According to Margaret, the pleading went as follows:

> *"But, why are you leaving us?"*
> *"There must be some way we can work this out together."*
> *"Give us another chance—we'll change—we'll offer you a competitive rate."*

"We promise."

"I was like—now?" says Margaret, incredulously. "Are you kidding me?"

RISING DEBT AND BANKRUPTCY

Americans are sinking deeper and deeper into debt. Defined as a percentage of the assets of the average American family, debt increased by 25 percent between 2001 and 2004. During that same period, the credit card debt of middle-class families rose 75 percent. In 2004, personal credit card debt in the United States reached $800 billion.[3]

These numbers are astounding. And yet, they are nothing compared to our national debt—that is, the debt owed by our government to the rest of the world. What we owe on our credit cards is a mere *tenth* of the $8.2 trillion that America owes to China, Japan, and a host of other countries.[4] In 2005, our nation's deficit—imagine a checking account overdraft for the nation—was $314 billion. When Bill Clinton left office, the United States had a surplus—extra money in the checking account—of $236 billion. Yet the Bush administration keeps on borrowing, more quickly than any other administration in our history. To Bush Republicans, a.k.a. "fiscal conservatives," the world is a limitless credit card.

When our government can't afford to make interest payments on their debt, the Treasury Department asks Congress for the equivalent of more credit. But what do you do when you can't take it, or don't have it, anymore? If you can, as an individual, you start over. You declare bankruptcy to erase your debts. It's something more corporations have done since Bush took office than during the entire rest of U.S. history combined (including during the Great Depression). Enron did it. So did WorldCom. United Airlines. Continental. Kmart. And a slew of others.

Nearly half of the middle-class families who filed for bankruptcy in 2001 (the same year Enron did) did so because they couldn't pay their medical bills. Enron did it because they lied (about pretty much everything) and got caught. Then their stock tanked and they couldn't pay their bills. But the problem is that it's easier for them than for you.

How has Congress tried to help these hard-up American families? By trying to make it tougher for these same people —but not for companies—to declare bankruptcy. They failed in 2002 when the Senate voted down a major bankruptcy reform bill, and again in March 2003. But on tax day, April 15, 2005, the House, with an expanded Republican majority, passed a bill ironically called the Bankruptcy Abuse Prevention and Consumer Protection Act of 2005.[5] The Senate, richer by four Republican seats after the 2004 election, followed suit.

During the Senate debate around the bill, the Republicans voted down every single consumer-friendly amendment. They voted *against* a provision assuring that old people who declare bankruptcy don't lose their homes. They voted *against* allowing seriously ill people to declare bankruptcy as a result of the cost of their illness. They voted *against* military service members and veterans being able to hold onto their homes in the case of bankruptcy, even when caused by ridiculous interest rates from predatory lenders—charged, for example, when they were *at war*. They voted *against* protecting employee pensions when corporations declare bankruptcy. In other words, they voted against every single item that would have helped the average citizen; at the same time, they voted for every emergency war addendum and tax cut for the wealthy.

You'll be happy to know, however, that the Republican senators did defeat an amendment that would have made it harder for the wealthy to declare bankruptcy. So really, they did stay true to the idea of the consumer protection part of the act—for *rich* consumers. Once the Senate passed the bill, Senate Majority Leader Bill Frist (R-Tennessee) applauded:

> *"This legislation restores personal responsibility and fairness to an abused system."*[6]

Six months later, Frist, the beacon of righteousness, was indicted on fraud charges.

Credit card companies give twice as much in political funds to Republicans as to Democrats. The issuers that lobbied congress included MBNA, Bush's biggest 2000 election-campaign donor, and a company which gave 85 percent of its contributions to Republicans.[7] When the Senate voted 74 to 25 for the bankruptcy reform bill favoring credit card issuers, it was the biggest rewrite of bankruptcy law in a quarter of a century.[8] Instantly, almost one million Americans a year were affected.

Meanwhile, Treasury Secretary John Snow was doing the only job he's had in the Bush administration—acting as debt front man to Congress. He has succeeded in making sure that the administration can keep racking up its own debt, even as it remains tremendously unhelpful regarding the debt, though paltry in comparison, of its own citizens. Since 2003, the country's debt level has increased a trillion dollars annually —not surprisingly, setting a new record high each year.[9] Secretary Snow warned Congress in mid-February 2006 that unless the government could borrow a trillion additional dollars from other countries, the *United States of America* might have to declare bankruptcy. This was Snow's third such warning to Congress; they began, not coincidentally, soon after the

Iraq war began and the first round of tax cuts for the rich took hold.

America has been in danger of going bankrupt for three of the five years Bush has been in office. Snow had to get Congress to raise the amount we borrowed, just so the United States could pay the *interest* on the money it keeps borrowing. Reckless, but true. In 2005 alone, the Bush administration spent $352 billion of your money on just the *interest* that it owes holders of our national debt. That's five times what it paid for education during that same time. If we were to break down this enormous figure, each American citizen has a share of its debt to the tune of $27,655.[10] That's the price of a brand new 2006 Ford Explorer.[11]

IS YOUR ATM/DEBIT CARD—LESS COSTLY?

To Abdel Hosni, a club manager in New York's East Village, who arrived here from Morocco with nothing in his wallet, it's his most important card.

"See this?"

he says, fingering its edges gently like they're made of fine crystal. He flips it over slowly.

"It's got three important uses."

I consider the number three. Most people told me their ATM card was the most important one because it linked them to their money.

"Look," he says, pointing the edge at me, "see how straight, how strong this is? There's no door I can't open with it.

Bathroom. Apartment. Front door. You lose a key, any key, and this baby," he holds up the card, "is your new key. And, it gets me my money."

"Got it," I nod. "So, what's the third?"

"It's my ID."

"But," I say, "There's no picture of you on it."

"Doesn't matter," he says. "You flash this thing quick and it works. I'm telling you, it's all about the attitude." He flashes a grin and pours me a drink. "Attitude," he repeats.

Attitude is something that banks have in spades. That's why they charge you fees to get access to *your* money. It used to be that states and cities had a say in that, but the finance industry has given more money to federal politicians than any other industry on the planet.[12] That means they get to override state and city laws.

An obscure federal agency in Washington called the Office of the Comptroller of the Currency (OCC) recently issued rules that took away even more state power over things like ATM fees. In January 2004, it decided, while no one was looking or caring, that it had sole legal authority to enforce consumer protection rules that applied to national banks (ones with "national" or "N.A." in their name).[13] This was despite the fact that Congress never said it could, because the Bush conservatives aren't really conservative about the ways in which ordinary Americans get their pockets pinched.

How annoying is it to pay a fee to get to your money, anyway? ATMs, or automated teller machines, have been around since the 1970s. Fees are more recent. Banks started imposing a fee on customers for using someone else's ATM in the mid-1980s. It was called a "foreign" or "off-us" fee. This became even more common in the following decade.

ATM fees hit record highs in 2005. "Wrong fees," as they are now commonly called, are the worst. That's when you get hit for using an ATM that doesn't belong to your bank when you take money out. Then—and you may not realize this, so check your statement—your own bank charges you a separate fee because you didn't get your money from them. Double jeopardy. At an average cost to you of $2.91 per withdrawal. Here's what kills me: the surcharge fee (the one just to pull your money out) averages $1.54.[14] The cost of each transaction to your bank is 27 cents.[15] Congress has not chosen to address this rather anti-consumer discrepancy during the Bush administration. As a result, in 2005 Americans paid $4.3 billion in withdrawal fees at ATMs not owned by their bank.

ALL THOSE OFFERS

Since the Diner's Card was created in 1950 to make life easier for traveling businessmen, Americans have been obsessed with credit cards. Once used for convenience purposes (to avoid paying cash) they have become our most common method of payment. In 2004, Visa booked record revenue of $2.4 billion. By the middle of 2005, more shoppers used Visa cards for purchases than the year before—up 17.5 percent over the year before.[16] More people borrowing also looks good for the U.S. economy, since consumer spending accounts for 70 percent of our gross domestic product. But that doesn't mean people are more financially stable.

Since Bush took office, the percentage of workers with employer-provided health insurance has gotten smaller, as has the maximum duration of unemployment benefits. The American savings rate is negative for the first time since World War II. Median household income has fallen every year. One out of three American households uses credit cards for basic living expenses like rent, groceries, or utilities. The average credit card debt for all families in America is $8,650.[17] And more than half of the households that use credit cards to cover basic needs have less than $1,000 in nonretirement savings.[18] Clearly, financial stability is becoming harder and harder to find. Ways to rack up debt, however, seem to greet us in our mailbox every day.

There are supposed to be rules that help keep the average American from vicious cycles of debt. These rules, called usury laws, were created to cap the rates of interest and types of fees creditors could charge. They came from values established by none other than three of the world's major religions—Christianity, Islam, and Judaism—which state that it is just plain wrong to profit by exploiting people's needs.[19] These laws were adopted after the American Revolution by the colonies and subsequently by all fifty states.

The federal government was supposed to supplement these laws. But instead, in 1978, came deregulation from Washington and the Federal Reserve. It allowed banks and creditors to get around those state rules for out-of-state customers.[20] Some moved their "credit headquarters" to states with fewer rules, like Delaware and South Dakota, so that most customers, by definition, lived out of state. Other cards are issued by "national" creditors that don't have to abide by state usury laws. There are no laws against those hefty late fees and increases in interest rates. Unless you switch cards or threaten to leave them, that rate never goes down. Credit card companies never send you glossy letters stating, "Good going! You've been such a great customer, we thought we'd *lower* your rate—just to say *thanx*."

Instead, you get endless promotions for new cards asking you to transfer your balance or "consolidate your debt" for six months at a lower rate, after which it will be hiked up again. In 2004, credit card companies sent out five billion solicitations. This works out to roughly 68 per household. That's a lot of mail.[21]

This barrage of mail has a purpose. The sad truth is that the credit card industry wants you in debt. They make money off the interest you pay them. And banks that offer you a line of credit are worse. First, they may charge you for a checking account and pay you about nothing in interest for a savings account. Say you deposit $100 in a savings account that offers 2 percent interest; you make $2 at the end of the year. The bank, on the other hand, turns around and lends your $100 to someone else by way of a card or loan. Say they charge this person 18 percent interest. The bank makes $18, pays you $2 and pockets the extra $16. If you borrow that $100 on your credit card at 18 percent interest, it would take 37 years paying the 2 percent minimum to be done with it.

Americans are immersed in a horrible cycle: banks and credit card companies make astounding amounts of money off of us, and use their power very effectively to influence decisions of our government, while the average citizen has a harder and harder time just paying his or her bills, let alone demanding that his or her government be accountable to him or her.

FAIRHOPE AND DREAMS

In mid-January, the town of Fairhope, Alabama, still has thin white strands of Christmas lights circling the trees along Main Street. Delicate bunches of flowers in patriotic colors mark the street corners. There, on a bright Saturday morning, I meet with Sonny Brewer, a 57-year-old author. We drink coffee at the community table in the Page and Palette, one of two independent bookstores in town (Sonny's is the other), and we are surrounded by friendly and welcoming faces.

Sonny's first novel, *The Poet of Tolstoy Park*, came out in March 2004. He's a warm man with a white beard and mustache, wearing an old brown leather jacket, black button shirt and jeans. He radiates passion as he talks of how recently his fortunes have changed; his book has just been optioned for a film and turned into a screenplay.

He grew up in rural Alabama, but moved to Fairhope in 1978.

> *"I knew when I got here, that I was home," he says. "My first novel is about Fairhope, so is my second. My third, too—the sun is brighter here, the nights are darker, and I hear the wind better."*

Sonny used to write the local newspaper's general interest column, which he called "Over the Transom."

> *"I was living on a boat before email existed and I'd literally have to crawl 'over the transom' to hand in my columns."*

It was a lifelong dream for Sonny to open his own bookstore. That dream came true when Over the Transom opened in 1997. Sonny says,

> *"I did it on a credit card in a heartbeat. I funded my bookstore on $3,500 out of a credit card advance."*

A few years ago, though, times were so tough that he feared he'd have to close his store. Then Fried Sweet Potato Queen Jill Comer Browne convinced him to sell something—

> *"that novel," she said, "you have nothing to lose."*

It was autobiographical, written for his sons, but he decided to give it a shot. That book didn't fly, but his agent asked him for another which did. The day before his meeting with a bankruptcy lawyer his agent informed him that Random House wanted to offer him a contract.

"That book deal saved my bookstore."

After about 20 minutes and a cinnamon latte, Sonny asks me,

"So after how much chatting do people usually wind up taking out their wallets?"

"About 20 minutes," I answer.

He takes his out. In his wallet he has a driver's license and no photos. He's one of the few people carrying a Social Security card; most fear identity theft.

"I don't care—my identity, they can have it,"

was his response, waving a hand. He even laminated it because it was getting old. Sonny also has one credit card, but no debit card. When he needs cash, he goes to the local bank. He has two—First Gulf and Colonial.

"I like to keep them competitive," he says, stroking his beard. "If I need cash, I just cash a check—the old-fashioned way."

Sonny Brewer now has no debt and pays his credit card balance every month. *Unlike the Bush administration.*

"They should shape credit cards like shovels, because you can dig a hole and can't get out. Like a grave. Why didn't I write a check then?"

he wonders aloud, referring to when he opened his bookstore.

"I didn't have the money, so you live dangerously— for a dream—you dig a hole with your little shovel."

Very much like the Bush administration.

Except the Bush gang has a much bigger shovel, and has already dug a longer lasting and deeper hole than any of us ever could. They are doing it with shovelfuls of the average American's financial security. Their dream, for middle- and lower-class America and its grandchildren, is more like a nightmare. Think Alice shooting down an infinite rabbit hole of poor choices and increasing debt. It's a whole lot more dangerous for the economy than opening a bookstore in an artsy village in Alabama.

Your Employee ID and the Gone Old Days

Detroit's not exactly a holiday destination. Unless you like damp chill and your favorite color is gray. Even if that's your thing, Detroit will disappoint. The late January skies are dull white. The snow flurries are noncommittal, like they can't be bothered to stick. They sort of disappear into the atmosphere, like many of the city's industries and jobs.

There used to be a billboard entering the city that tallied the number of American cars coming off assembly lines each minute. But now, who wants to point out failure? Today the only similar one is on Interstate 405 in Southern California—it counts the gallons of gas saved driving Toyota hybrids. Driving downtown, I pass gleaming Super Bowl XL banners. Everywhere. They're welcoming the burst of visitors, mostly ridiculously rich businessmen and celebrities that will pack hotels for a minute and drink tons of Bud.

My taxi driver's a 20-year-old Indian guy named Monty. He's studying for his high school GED, after getting mixed up with the wrong crowd first time 'round. As he explains:

"Tony's doing time for threatening to kill his girlfriend while packing. Rob had two kids with this chick and is trying to straighten himself out. Mark got done for crack possession."

Monty lists this string of accomplishments like they are no big deal, the kind of stuff he sees every day. After all, this is Detroit, circa 2006.

During the 1970s, the largest of the big three automakers, GM, was still riding high off its post–World War II heyday. It was the leading employer in America outside the federal government. It provided workers full benefits, thanks to union-negotiated contracts. The United Auto Workers union sprouted four decades earlier, just after FDR brought the New Deal to an America trying to escape the Great Depression. The UAW was born in Detroit. At its peak in 1978 it had 1.5 million members; union membership is now down to 640,000.[1]

Jerry Fisher is one of them. He carries his UAW retirement card with pride in his wallet. Before retiring in June 2004, Fisher was elected or appointed President of Staff Council of the UAW, GM Section, every year for 43 years. Though done with the plants, you can tell he "works it" like a rock star from behind the scenes: he seems just as connected to the daily goings on, both with workers and to management decisions, as during his union tenure. As we walk through the corridors of the Dave Miller Building on East Jefferson Avenue, a procession of people smile and wave at him:

"Hey Mayor!" "Hey Fish!"

Jerry is a really big guy. Take an X-Large and add a few Xs, and you get the idea. He's a warm guy, the kind who listens more than he speaks, but totally knows what's up. The kind you'd want in your corner. Today he's sporting a huge leather jacket: red, white, blue, and silver, and in huge letters, "XL Super Bowl, Detroit, February 5, 2006." Underneath it, he's wearing a bright red checkered shirt and white pants. As we leave the building for lunch at nearby Sinbad's on the river, more greetings follow him. There's camaraderie amongst these men, the kind that comes from spending 30 to 40 years together on the assembly line.

"Hey Fish—couldn't stay away?"

Up the street, in front of Solidarity House—UAW's international headquarters—stands a bronzed statue: *The Builder.* Sculptured biceps bulge under hiked-up shirt sleeves. His hair looks like it could wave in the wind, like it'd be dirty blond and sexy. He is poised. And for a piece of metal, he's pretty damn hot. *The Builder* comes from a time when it was cool to be blue collar, when it was accepted that people worked for wages *and* benefits, for today's money and tomorrow's security. An era when it wasn't considered greedy or inconvenient to demand fair treatment and compensation in return for putting your time and sweat into the corporate till.

Over the years, that has changed. As the bulges grew in the pockets of CEOs, so too did the idea that workers were collateral damage, tools—not people—that could be "restructured" as needed. Any sense of modesty in the upper ranks was replaced by a terminal case of entitlement.

"CEOs are more worried about shareholders than workers. If you had stock during Clinton—who, yeah, had a bit of a

*zipper problem—you made money. There was less national
debt. Employment was higher,"says Jerry.*

The pay gap between senior executive and lower rung
worker has exploded. Bush accepted more corporate campaign
donations during his 2004 campaign than any other administration ever.[2] Once Bush's team of "conservatives" re-secured
the Oval Office, they voted in the most sweeping set of
corporate tax breaks in two decades.[3] As liberal as they were
with corporations, they remained conservative when it came
to individuals (those not running corporations), and have
remained silent through continued reductions in employee
benefit plans. Their vision of individual responsibility is the
kind that results in employees bearing more responsibility for
health and retirement expenses while corporate execs get to
pocket a heftier chunk of the profits.

Our president talks a good game about the strength of
each American, but his brand of "individualism" means more
personal prosperity for the ones who can afford it. In this
scenario, most Americans—the builders, the Jerry Fishers
amongst us—are ignored. We are seen by our own government as a relic, no more than statues that should be melted
down in the pursuit of a better—read: economically unequal
—tomorrow.

I don't want to overromanticize the past; I wasn't there to
feel it. When the UAW was born after the New Deal, there
certainly was not a perfect balance between employee and
employer. But the power and unity of a larger and coordi-
nated workforce happened to coincide, particularly in the
auto industry, with greater strength for both the auto industry and the workforce. And despite the economic growing
pains of these previous generations, there was a feeling—in
short supply today—that the American worker was valued.

SO, WHAT'S HAPPENING TO THE JOBS?

Jerry shakes his head as we sit in the staff room in the Dave Miller building up the road from the Solidarity House. He leans against a table filled with papers, books, and empty water bottles, and laments,

"The administration says they've created millions of jobs, but—where are they?"

In his 2006 State of the Union address, Bush claimed that 4.6 million jobs had been created during his presidency. They're definitely not in manufacturing. Since Bush took office, almost 3 million manufacturing jobs have been lost, mostly overseas and across borders.[4]

Born in Pontiac, Michigan, Jerry's blood pumps auto:

"My grandpa and dad worked in auto. My mom worked at Pontiac during WWII."

Fish graduated from Avondale High School in 1955.

"Back then," he says, "all you had to do was walk over to a nearby GM plant and apply."

Since 1959, he's built everything from Greyhound buses, which GM no longer produces there, to city buses, which it also eliminated from production, to heavy- and medium-duty trucks. GM has since phased out heavy duty to their plants in Mexico and Canada, and medium to Flint.

There's a lot to be pissed about. Manufacturing jobs are leaving faster than *American Idol* contestants. Wages and benefits have decreased relative to hours on the job, unless you're a zillionaire.[5] Corporations say that health insurance is either too expensive or unavailable, or they use it as a reason to keep wages down. Guaranteed pensions—once the bedrock of America's blue-collar worker—are fast disappearing. The alternative, ardently supported by Bush and his clan—who extol the virtues of lean government, while liberally bloating it with debt and doling out corporate tax breaks like they're going out of style—is to roll the 401(k) dice in the stock market.

GM and Ford have been relocating car and truck production to Canada like mad, where there's national health care. The CAW (Canadian Auto Workers) union broke away from the UAW in the 1980s. At the time, it had 150,000 members. That number has doubled. John Truffa, former Treasurer of Council for International Harvesters-Navistar (a companion union to the UAW), retired in 2000. But his forehead still wrinkles when he discusses the prospects of the country's manufacturing industry:

> *"I'm not sure corporations can turn it around without the government's help."*

John, a longtime organizer, is a mild-mannered man who gets passionate when discussing issues that impact American workers.

> *"Here, if we get increases in wages, it goes right to health care," says John. "So, I think trade policy is a big problem; our government doesn't manage it, or even talk about it."*

That's because they're hoping we don't really understand it. Bush has created the biggest trade imbalance in our country's history, while not talking about it. This means we import more items than we export, and the cost of us importing all those goods is higher than the profits we make from selling products to other countries. Bush could create a more insular trade policy. He could, for example, place a wage differential tax on goods produced elsewhere, to make up for the fact that other countries can produce items more cheaply since they pay workers less. (Many UAW workers say this would help them compete with more cheaply made parts and vehicles coming in from outside the United States.) But it ain't gonna happen.

Bush does say quite often that he believes in the gods of global competition and has no intention of helping the auto, or any other, transportation industry. It doesn't help that American cars have taken a backseat to Japanese ones. Toyota's gunning for GM's number one spot—based on the number of cars sold worldwide—and is gaining fast.[6]

In early 2006, GM continued to not help their workers: they announced 30,000 layoffs and the closing of 12 facilities in the United States.[7] Ford joined in with 25,000 job cuts. The reason reported by most of the mainstream media is that health and pension benefits are killing the companies. Basically, former workers are refusing to die more quickly. What most people and the media have ignored is that management was asleep at the wheel.

"GM and Ford just didn't make changes fast enough," says John. "They were too in love with themselves." Jerry explains: "They should have involved plant workers in the process. We could have told them what they need to do to make cars people wanted to buy, but they wouldn't listen. Instead, they cut benefits, instead of focusing on making and selling better cars."

Jacked

Concerning the media furor over benefits, Jerry says,

"We're not being greedy about that stuff. A pension is a wage increase we didn't get, that's all—people should see that."

According to John,

"The bottom line is that we can't compete with countries with national health care or no minimum wage. The government isn't addressing this. You don't need a government that doesn't serve its citizens—what the hell's the point?"

We have slipped very far from that point in just a few short years. John raised four kids with a wife not working and full health benefits for the family on a union wage. Jerry raised five. He puts it simply:

"You just felt secure—everyone was together back then."

For people living on minimum wage, it's even worse. Minimum wage is now the average salary for a third of the private sector. It has the lowest purchasing power in 50 years.[8] House Republicans have voted down increases since 1997, when it was last raised from $4.75 to $5.15 an hour. The argument goes—if we raise the minimum wage, our workers will have to get paid more. (So greedy of them!) Then it'll be even more attractive to send jobs to Mexico and India where workers get paid less. This way, our workers can make less *and* their jobs can go to Mexico and India.

The other alternative, which might please this screwy conservative logic, would be to take the minimum wage down to 50 cents an hour. Then we could really compete with Mexico. By January 2006, seventeen states and the District of Columbia decided to raise their minimum wage, since the federal government hasn't.[9] Blue states, to be exact. One of the only red states with a minimum wage higher than the fed's is Florida.

THE SAME EVERYWHERE

Similar stories came from all the major auto cities I visited. A week earlier, in Oklahoma City, I met with David Dunn and Terry Clary at an office complex of single story dirt-brown buildings along a stretch of land that redefined "flat." Terry, an amalgamated local union president, represents employees for 19 different companies that feed from the car manufacturing industry. Dressed in everything denim—jean button-down shirt, jean pants, and a maroon cap with the Local 286 logo—he's got piercing blue eyes, and two daughters who finished high school with, as he puts it,

"no decent job prospects."

David Dunn is president of nonamalgamated UAW Region 5. He's a burly guy, bald with a gray and brown streaked goatee. The Oklahoma GM plant was slated to be the first of 12 plants to close by 2008. According to David, in a late act of desperation Oklahoma's governor, Brad Henry, offered GM $200 million of incentives to stay in the city. GM basically replied,

"No thanx, we're good."

GM management might not have been efficient at modifying their cars to be more desirable, but they were damn efficient at keeping to their plant closings schedule. On February 20,

2006, the Oklahoma City factory produced its last car, and shut its doors to 2,400 workers.[10]

Two hundred million dollars was too little, too late to keep GM's plant from closing. Though the auto industry was once such an important component of the American economy, and our country's personality, there was no congressional or presidential outcry. No call from our elected officials to save the day, even though they are very good at lining up to save money for those that have the most of it.

"Bush only knows one song—tax cuts for the rich," says David. "Before the Great Depression, seven out of eight presidents were Republican. They drove this country to the ground by 1929. Finally, you had a Democrat with FDR. It was more than 20 years before another Republican president was elected. They destroyed the economy of this country once and they're doing it again."

"For us, it's disheartening," sighs Terry. "I have units on the Mexican border, U.S. side. They were making $6 an hour before we negotiated their contract. Now, they're at $12 an hour. But Mexican jobs are making $1 an hour. Tops. We can't compete with that. We should at least tax imports relative to these wage differences."

David registered as a Democrat to vote in primaries. For him, as for others across the country, voting is about who's listening to his issues. It's also about considering who understands where he's coming from. At the moment, he's pretty uninspired by the lack of connection the Bush conservatives have to his life.

"The present administration in DC were born rich and are gonna die rich," says David. "When I vote, you know what I

do? I ask—did this person ever know what it's like to be like me? When I was a kid, my dad could buy five hamburgers for a dollar. There were four of us; do the math, nobody got two."

As far as he's concerned, if today's political leaders didn't ever sit at the same kind of dinner table, they don't have a clue how to represent him.

DOWNSIZING EVERYTHING

It's not just auto manufacturing that's been downsized in terms of people and benefits. It's corporate America everywhere. When I was a little kid in the late '70s, Poughkeepsie, New York, was to IBM as Detroit, Michigan, was to GM. Our parents were engineers, plant managers, mainframe technicians. We didn't have the slightest idea what they did, but we were aware of what being a "beamer" meant. It meant we went to the IBM country club for weekend picnics or to watch the IBM fireworks on July 4th. There was no such thing as changing jobs or being laid off. Our doctors were paid by IBM. Our dentists were, too.

By the early 1980s, internal IBM budgets were slashed and the workforce was quietly reduced from 370,000 to 260,000. But not by massive layoffs—that came in the early '90s. It was by early retirements and departmental consolidations.

IBM paid health insurance until the mid-'90s. Then it assessed a "co-payment" of $180 per month for a family plan. That went gradually up to $320 per month in 2001. Deductibles rose to $500 annually. My dad's job and my dad ultimately escaped, like many others, to Mexico.

It used to be that people got paid less in exchange for more benefits. Today, they get paid less for fewer. It used to be that companies took care of future risk. Today, we do. More and more, pensions and health care are the chips on the table to keep other employee benefits (like pay) in check.

Corporate pensions used to be part of what employees could count on in their old age, topped off with Social Security and Medicare guaranteed by the government, and health care packages for life from their companies. Old-school pension plans (called "defined benefit" or "DB" plans) promised employees fixed monthly payments upon retirement, no matter what. Over the past 20 years, employers decided they didn't want to make promises. They started offering "defined-contribution programs" where employers and employees contribute to a pot that gives fluctuating monthly payments on retirement.

After WWII, 62 percent of American employees had full pensions covered by their companies. It was down to 13 percent in 1997. Some companies, like Hewlett Packard, replaced traditional pension plans with 401(k) plans. Others, like United Airlines, just stopped paying them. Public workers, 90 percent of whom still have traditionally defined benefit plans —namely because 37 percent are in unions—are next at risk.

More and more, pensions and health care are used as bargaining tools to keep other employee benefits (like pay) in check. At giant companies like IBM and Verizon, pension freezes have been spreading like the flu; also contagious is the trend of replacing their future pension plans with 401(k) plans. But study after study has shown that people who barely make ends meet in the first place have a lot harder time socking extra money away in their 401(k)s. Plus, there is no guarantee that returns will be there when we need them; do we really want to subject the retirement of Americans to market volatility?

This trend's a perfect example of Bush's vision of an "ownership society." You own your retirement, you own the risk.

It's not your company's problem. Similarly, Social Security shouldn't be the government's problem; neither should health care. Maybe they should get out of the highway and postal businesses while they're at it. Or, maybe, they're just plain wrong.

Saving for your own retirement and health care is rather hard when you can't feed your family or pay your bills. Luckily, that's what President Bush's tax cuts are for, right? Wrong. Just take a look at their damage. The cost of the cuts he passed between 2001 and 2005 was equal to two-thirds of the country's 2005 deficit.[11] And for most Americans, these tax cuts haven't even put any extra money in their wallets. On average, we've received about $600 a family. Yet, as we all feel too keenly, gas, tuition, health insurance, and medical expenses rose much more.

Meanwhile, corporations have been raking in more and more tax breaks under the Bush administration. Before 1916, individuals didn't pay any federal income tax—companies footed the entire bill. After World War II, corporations paid half of the cost of running the government. By 2003, they weren't so supportive: their share had shriveled to a paltry 7 percent.[12]

Six out of ten companies don't pay any federal income tax —and not because they're using that extra money to get out there and hire new people or pay workers more for their labor. No, they're paying executives more. Every U.S. industry increased what it paid CEOs in 2004.[13] It was highest in the construction industry, where the average CEO bags $2.8 million a year (though many make much more than that) and lowest in transportation, mostly because the airlines are doing too poorly for CEOs to get away with it. That said, Doug Parker, CEO of US Airways (which went bankrupt twice since 2002), was paid well above average in 2005, with his $5.8 million check.[14] In 2004, the average CEO got paid 32 times more than the average worker. The top people at Fortune 500 companies got an average pay raise of 54 percent.[15] You did, too—right?

THE MILITARY AS ORGANIZED LABOR

Baker, California, is 95 miles from the glitzy Las Vegas strip, off the Interstate 15 highway that cuts through Death Valley. Its one road is home to the infamous Mad Greek Diner (drive south from the strip—you can't miss the signs). A favorite haunt for truckers, who get free drinks there, and the people of Fort Irwin Military Base, it correctly boasts the best strawberry milkshakes—ever. Seriously, they're amazing.

I was going to meet Officer Jimmy Lee and his family at the base, but they welcomed the opportunity for a shake. The base itself is small, but maneuvers take place in an area the size of the state of Rhode Island. Soldiers train there in mock Iraqi villages, before heading for the real thing.

Jimmy is 32 years old. He served in Iraq in the "initial push" of early 2003. For his activities on March 22 of that year, while Company Commander of the 3rd Infantry Division, he was awarded a Silver Star. He told me that his was one of about 150 awarded so far in Iraq and Afghanistan. He received a Bronze one shortly afterwards. He's a dedicated soldier, husband, and father. He fights for the country and provides for his loved ones.

Defense Secretary Donald Rumsfeld is no Jimmy Hoffa. But the military has the kind of employment package that makes union leaders salivate. They've enjoyed decent wage increases over the Bush years. But their retirement and health benefits may be next on the chopping block.

The men and women of our military are noticing this possible shift. It's not about whether any war is right or wrong, or about patriotism, or serving one's country. It's about their wallets. It's about the future of their families.

Jimmy Lee and his wife, Carrie, grew up in neighboring North Carolina towns. Married 13 years, they have two beautiful sons, Kiser and Gralen. When Carrie went into labor with Gralen, there was a hospital seven miles away from their North Carolina base, but they had to drive 25 miles to one that accepted the military's insurance provider, TRICARE. They did this in rush hour traffic and on a backed up Interstate 85. When they finally reached the hospital, the attending nurse urged,

> *"Don't push, the doctor's not in yet." Says Carrie, "He walked in just in time. I mean, you can't hold back on your second."*

Jimmy doesn't believe in national health care, but he does think that things could be different and that we need a better overall strategy. One suggestion that had been batted around was putting the military under Medicare because it's accepted in more places. The Lee's and families like them, even with the comparably better coverage the military provides, face other problems, like whether retirement benefits will stay solid. Chances are they won't, even for the military. Jimmy's been in the service for 13 years.

> *"Seven more and I can retire. In the old days you got a steady pension, but now the military is thinking along other lines, like 'we should give them more money now and let them invest it themselves.'"*

Jimmy sips his shake:

> *"It's small talk now, but . . . military pensions are a good thing, we appreciate better retirement and less pay, but, there's*

been talk . . . of change . . . these new plans—TSPs
[Thrift Savings Plans]—are becoming more popular."

That means the military may be on the hook for its own retirement in the future.

He is worried by these ideas of self-investment.

"I personally like the way it is now, the pension—it's
guaranteed and the market isn't guaranteed. I can't sit
around and watch the market and trade. I don't have
the time and energy to put into it."

The more the military shoves retirement investment responsibility on our country's soldiers, like corporations have done
to their employees, the more they will need to face the
risks and time consumption of self-investment like the rest of
the country. Even our military isn't gonna remain safe from
these risks if the Bush conservatives march on. I don't know
about you, but I don't think our military should be spending their time talking to Merrill Lynch brokers. The defense
budget is too big for that kind of waste of our military's time
and focus.

No one would accuse our country, with the largest army
and military budget in the world, of being socialist. Amazingly,
military benefits pretty much are. Our military has decent
pension and health-care packages. And they should. So should
the auto workers, the Wal-Mart workers, and everyone else.
This fundamental security is what made us competitive in the
world.

We are all in danger of losing that security. Every time
Bush opens his mouth about democracy overseas and cuts a
social benefit back home. Every time he wags a finger at the
Social Security system and advocates health savings accounts,

instead of a national health plan that will help American workers compete on a global scale. We need to return to an America where workers are proud to show off their employee ID cards—and where the government actually cares about the well-being of its citizens.

4

Your Student ID and Educating America

The rest of Texas may be red, but Austin, the capitol, has its own ideas about how the country should work. One is plastered on a bumper sticker: *Please make the scary Republicans go away.*

Austin Java is a favorite hangout of UT (University of Texas) students. It offers an assortment of vital caffeine items, smoothies, and pretty decent food. Over tortilla chips, salsa, and Monterey Jack quesadillas, I talk with four UT students, all of whom also work with children at the YMCA under the supervision of my sister-in-law, Marisol, herself a UT graduate and first-generation Mexican-American. These students all value their student identification cards. Here and around the country, the student ID gets thousands of kids into their dorms, maybe a free pass to an art museum, and cafeteria food of varying quality. But unfortunately, the student ID also brings with it an increasingly painful price tag.

A record number of students graduated high school in 2006. College enrollment is projected to increase by 14 percent over the next decade. Four out of five of those additional students will be minorities.[1] Half of them will come from the Hispanic community, like these young women.

Vanessa Sweet is studying for her second bachelor's degree, in biology, having received her first in Spanish. The third of four siblings, she's a first-generation college student. Her mom dropped out of elementary school and dad finished middle school in Mexico.

Her family got their citizenship in 1992.

"Dad was in the army six years and later got certified as an electrician. He's been working twenty-five years as an electrician in a South Houston oil refining company. He's the only money maker in the family. Mom's a diabetic."

She has cornflower eyes and is wearing a green shirt over a black tank top. Her hair is bobbed and auburn.

"I got a Texas Excellence Grant that covers tuition. I was a Texas Scholar and also got $100 per semester in Pell Grants."

(The largest federal grant program, Pell Grants are generally awarded to families who make less than $30,000 a year, critical in helping lower income students get to college.[2])

"I was never offered work study, though I always applied. I worked all the time, 'cause I didn't want my parents paying; they'd done enough,"

says Vanessa, fingering her silver heart necklace.

House Republicans decided not to increase Pell Grants when they had the opportunity at the end of 2005. Pells have been frozen at $4,050 per year since Bush took office. They are worth $900 less today, adjusted for inflation, than they were in the 1970s.

Sitting to Vanessa's left is Angelica Garcia. She's a Spanish literature major, and also the first generation in her family to go to college. Her Mom is from El Salvador and worked as a housekeeper for one family for 20 years. Now she works at a coffee company. Her father came to the States from Mexico when he was 13. He has owned a bunch of Latino bars in Houston.

*"They were the places to go for the immigrant crowd,"
she explains.*

Angelica grew up in Magnolia, one of Houston's Hispanic neighborhoods.

"There are lots of immigrants and first-generation people there. At my elementary school, the first language was Spanish; I was an ESL student until sixth grade."

Her English is perfect. She is voluptuous, shy but intense, with big brown eyes, dark glasses, long stringy dark hair, and a nose ring. Her boyfriend sits at a table behind us pretending to read, but strains to catch bits of the conversation.

"I wound up getting a $10,000 Houston Rodeo scholarship by writing an essay about what I saw myself doing in the future," she says. "It's always been me and my mom—my dad's there, but not really there, you know. I wrote about her struggles just for me."

Angelica's drive and intelligence got her another scholarship, through a UT minorities program called CONNEXUS, of $1,000 per semester, as well as a Pell Grant and a grant from the state of Texas. Her work-study job was a math tutor for ESL students at Travis High School, which has a high proportion of minorities.

Bush likes math, too. That's why he told the nation he'd improve the quality of math and science education and teachers in his 2006 State of the Union address. It was a generous offer, except that his own math was off. Financial support for education technology in the nation's schools was slashed almost in half by the 2006 House budget.[3]

To my right, sipping ice water while I down the tortilla chips, is Indira Castillo. She's studying kinesiology and athletic training. Born in Nicaragua, she made the dean's list this year, saying,

"My parents were really pleased with that."

Her father graduated from a university in Nicaragua, applied for a Fulbright scholarship, went to the University of Pittsburgh, then to UT,

"knowing the slimmest amount of English,"

she explains. After a year, she and her mom joined him. The family lived in student housing for years.

"Mom was a maid, a Pizza Hut delivery person, and other things to support us."

Her father continued on for his Ph.D. in Latin American studies and Mom got a BA at UT.

"The whole time, my parents were crazy about education and fighting legal battles to be able to travel in the U.S. on student visas."

She is stunning, with ginger-brown hair, sharp eyes, and perfect features set in light caramel skin.

"I didn't qualify for financial aid, just a $1,000 Stafford Loan last year. During summers, I worked at Dell for $9.90 an hour and overtime of $14.85 an hour."

At which point, the other girls chirp in:

"$14.85!? Wow! Can we get jobs there?"

Indira traces the zipper of her hot-pink sweatshirt with her French-manicured nails.

"My parents are still paying Dad's school loans,"

she says with a worried face.

"My dad's fourth-generation Mexican," says Regina Campos, a Latin American studies major. "He's also doing his Ph.D. and paying loans. I got a job at the Y to help out—it's too much for them."

Two silver rings pierce her lips. She has raven hair with blunt bangs, and her eyes are coal black.

"My mom is very white. She works at a church in Tarrytown, one of the wealthy 'hoods, where houses are ridiculously huge— they could put like 40 people in each one."

Jacked

Regina is proud of her heritage and politically active in the Chicano student movement group, MEChA, that works with immigrant workers, including the janitorial and custodial staff at UT.[4]

"I grew up in a really white town, outside Austin—one of five Mexican kids at school. There was one black kid, no Asians. Everyone there was upper middle class, white, wealthy Republicans—I had different politics."

In no small part because of her intense commitment, Regina received a $1,000 scholarship for graduating high school early, plus a $1,400 scholarship from the League of United Latin American Citizens.[5] Her parents also took out Stafford and Parent Plus loans for her. Around the same time, the latest House education budget, recognizing the importance of those loan programs, raised interest rates on both of them.[6]

Unfortunately, these remarkable ladies are in very, very good company. Financial barriers keep almost half of college-qualified graduates from low income families from going to a four-year college, and almost a quarter from attending any college at all.[7] It's not too different for students from homes making less than $50,000. With average costs for one year at a public university around $13,000, it's no wonder so many families struggle to pay.[8]

If you're black or Hispanic, you have an even tougher time than if you're white. Says Angelica,

"Lots of people in my neighborhood look at the tuition numbers and think there's no way for them. It's discouraging for Latinos and minorities who want to come to school—and it's very discouraging that it's $13,000 to $17,000 a year."

Cost is one reason why the gap in college enrollment keeps growing, even as more minorities are graduating high school.[9] In 2005, college tuition and fees increased 7.1 percent for public four-year universities and 5.9 percent for private ones. Since Bush took office, both public and private have increased by a total of 34 percent, or $3,400 a year.[10] Since, on average, college-qualified minority students come from lower income families compared to white students, these increases in costs are even harder for them to swallow. Plus, these lower income students are even more dependent on loans that are harder to get and more difficult to pay off.

But getting a college education is not supposed to be this difficult. Even the federal government acknowledged this, when they first passed the Higher Education Act in 1965. It aimed to give every American, no matter what their financial condition, the ability to go to college.[11] Congress can revisit the bill every six years, looking at everything from student loans to Pell Grants to other forms of aid.

In their most recent look at the bill, our legislators worked hard. To offset the highest deficit *ever*, the House Committee on Education and the Workforce proposed the biggest cuts to educational programs *ever*. On November 18, 2005, in the dead of night—actually, just before 2 AM— the Committee passed a version of the bill that would chop higher education programs by $14.3 billion over a five-year period. The House then approved it on a narrow party line vote (212 to 206), with nine Republicans and one Independent joining the 196 Democrats that opposed the bill.[12]

After Thanksgiving break, the bill moved to the Senate. Four days before Christmas, Vice President Dick Cheney returned from a trip to the Middle East (safe to say, it was for something about war or oil) to cast the tie-breaking vote. Education lost. The bill returned to the House with some minor adjustments—that cut programs even further—and was re-approved in January 2006. It froze Pell Grants, and cut 21st Century Community Learning centers, Head Start, and other educational programs.

Of course, not everyone in this country needs financial aid for college; only four out of five students do, a mere 16 million people.[13] Others have millionaire parents.

"I was one of two Hispanic kids in Tarrytown. I'd go to school all raggedy dressed, they had designer clothes. I went to Austin High, where the Bush daughters went,"

says Indira.

Regina responds:

"I saw one UT student driving a Hummer; I don't even have a car."

"It's obvious people who live in wealthy dorms have rich parents," adds Indira. "I have friends who live in $9K a year apartments, so I know their parents are paying."

Angelica interjects,

"My mom, bless her, all her earnings she's giving me. It's hard. I can't call my parents and ask them for money to go to school."

"Lots of students grew up with money and shop like they aren't in college: Saks, Neiman Marcus. I thought The Gap was expensive. Like, there are $200 jeans?"

says Indira.

"My roommate buys $200 jeans,"

says Regina, rolling her eyes.

PORTLAND, OREGON

I fell in love with Portland, Oregon, the minute we met. It was the week before Christmas. U2 was performing their last concert of 2005 at the Rose Garden; Kanye West opened. Maybe it was the charming architecture of the downtown buildings, or the fog over the river, or the free trolleys. Or the fact that it had better coffee than Seattle.

But it was the people that really got to me—one in particular—the amazing De Ette Peck. She's a single mom and student at Mount Hood Community College. Having been a waitress for 15 years, she's now studying to become a community field nurse.

> *"Blood fascinates me," she explains to me during a phone conversation.*
>
> *"She's a freak!" shouts a young girl in the background.*
>
> *"That would be my 13-year-old daughter, Mikayla," she says.*

De Ette's my new hero. In addition to raising two girls with a full-time course load, she's a volunteer at the Oregon Food Bank, Head Start, and the Poverty Advisory Committee (PAC), and she works with the Portland Women's Crisis Center.

At 35, her life makes Erin Brockovich's seem like Paris Hilton's. The only girl of five, her mom was an alcoholic and a prescription drug user and her father was abusive. She was molested by a housekeeper at age six. Right after she graduated high school, she got involved in another violent relationship. The marriage started out as controlling but grew more physical. De Ette would have left, but nature intervened. She stuck with it after discovering she was pregnant. Mikayla was six months old before De Ette knew what she had to do.

"We got into a fight," she explains, "while I was holding her. That was the turning point."

After leaving her husband and undergoing an abortion, she met Trevor and got pregnant with her second daughter, Harleah Quinn. They wed two years later. Nine months afterwards, he raped her.

"All those suppressed memories from childhood came back. I went off the deep end." Reading my mind, she says, "Something out of Jerry Springer, isn't it?"

Soon after that conversation, I got to spend an evening with De Ette, her two daughters, Julia Massa, a public policy advocate, and Cassandra Garrison, Public Policy Director at the Oregon Food Bank. During an evening of pouring rain—or standard midwinter Portland weather—we gathered in McMenamins Courtyard Restaurant, at The Kennedy School in Northeast Portland. First built as an elementary school in 1915, it has been transformed into a guesthouse and eating spot complete with a series of cozy bars and a working brewery. The place smells of warm history and burnt oak.

Cassandra, as various media reports portray her, is "a pit bull for the poor." She looks anything but. With a wool sweater draped around her shoulders, dark curly hair, creamy skin and glasses, she looks more like a librarian or kindergarten teacher. At the age of 30 she was homeless with a child. Now 50, she prides herself on having busted all stereotypes of "The Welfare Mom." While living in shelters and Section Eight housing for years, she studied to be a civil engineer and eventually got a master's degree in public administration. That didn't keep poverty at bay for her, though. Through the Food Bank, she helps women navigate the welfare system, and gives inspiration to people like De Ette.

We begin our evening with some wine (well, actually, just me). De Ette's daughters are downing Shirley Temples, and she has a big test the next day. From appetizers of hummus and pita we move onto entrees, which include the fresh mozzarella and basil pizza of the week (again, that was me). The other crowd favorite is the BLT sub, a McMenamin's specialty along with their ruby ales.

It's been a tough slog for De Ette. Getting an education was an uphill battle against the welfare system. After Clinton's 1996 welfare reform, which was put into effect by the state of Oregon in 1998, you had to go from welfare directly to work, instead of getting an education. That meant going from one dead end job to another.

"The system doesn't always work for the underdog," she says. "If my kids were daycare age, I wouldn't get financial help for going to school myself."

Fortunately, single parents get more financial aid than other single people. Through the federal grant program that she applies for every year, De Ette gets $5,000 in loans and $4,400 in work-study. Plus, she receives $500 in child support. The rest of the $15,000 she needs each year comes from grants and scholarships.

De Ette jumped into advocacy with more jazz than the Energizer bunny. Her expertise is in the gray area of the working poor—families who make too much for subsidies but not enough to escape poverty. Since she never had an opportunity for education-related daycare when her kids were younger, she decided that others should. So, she joined a grant committee at her college and helped write a $25,000 grant for students to have daycare. She then raised $15,000 towards the effort. All in a day's work for De Ette. She smiles and says that she wants to create a bumper sticker that reads: *When I leave poverty I want to take as many people with me as I can.*

While talking, De Ette twists an index finger through her tousled honey-blond hair. Her huge blue-gray eyes are warm and tough. Her energy is contagious. She's got balls, the kind that the Democrats should look into getting.

"My other 'baby' is Head Start," she explains. "I'm very angry about the federal cut. If it wasn't for Head Start, I wouldn't be what I am today. My daughters graduated from Head Start. If we could implement their policies into public schools, we wouldn't have the problems with today's youth— they can change whole families."

If the Bush Republicans feel for people like De Ette Peck, they sure don't put that compassionate conservatism into financial action. On December 14, 2005, the House approved a bill that cut $800 million from the No Child Left Behind and Head Start programs. Since President Bush signed the No Child Left Behind law in 2002, he and the "education-friendly" Republicans have underfunded the law by $40 billion compared to what was authorized.[14] Head Start programs have been forced to choose amongst helping fewer children, firing employees, or cutting services. The cut to Head Start means it will service 32,000 fewer preschoolers and 2,300 fewer infants and toddlers in 2006 compared to 2005.[15] Though the number of working single moms has increased, the Child Care and Development Block Grant, which subsidizes child care expenses for low-income women, has been frozen since Bush took office, and will be cut in half in 2006.[16] Like so many of the people I spoke with, Cassandra sounded a common chord:

"We're funding the wrong programs, like giving tax breaks to the top 1 percent of the nation—and we're taxing me instead of corporations."

De Ette has a brilliant, and uniquely single mom, solution. She says,

> *"I'm frustrated with the government because of the waste going on. If they took frugal moms like me, we'd figure it out—I can make a dollar stretch a lot longer than the government."*

The passion of these two women is incredible. Despite their intensely busy lives, and relentless financial challenges, they shine when talking about their goals. De Ette manages to text her boyfriend, supervise her kids doing homework, and remain completely involved in the conversation. The federal government could learn a few things about getting things done from people like her.

Bush and his fellow conservatives could also learn a great deal about how to address those at the bottom of the money food chain.

> *"There's a difference between empathy and sympathy, you know. You don't want someone's pity,"* comments De Ette. *"That's why we fight for better priorities."*

As De Ette shoots off another text message, Cassandra comments:

> *"During the time I spent homeless,"* says Cassandra, *polishing off her BLT, "I discovered community organizing, to get people empowered and engaged. With education and knowledge, we can rock policy from the ground up."*

De Ette needs to leave early to prepare for her exam. As she scoops up her bag and makes sure her daughters have everything, I wonder what it'll be like for these girls when they try to get a college education if the current conservatives stay in power in Washington. She hugs me goodbye with a final thought about how government programs should be viewed:

"They're investing in me, and you know what? I'm a great investment!"

Damn straight she is.

5

Your Health Insurance Card and Caring for America

I had never taken an Aquacise class in my life. Nor had it ever occurred to me that I should. That changed when Jeanette Flom suggested I attend the one she taught at the Interbay YMCA in Tampa, Florida. Locating my black Speedo from beneath the piles of New York winter clothes, I accepted her invitation and left for the sunny Southeast corner of the country.

And then, there I was, with a group of ten senior women, all wearing multicolored cloth hats: pale pinks, mauves, periwinkles, lime greens. (I don't have a hat.) Together, we tiptoe into the 82-degree outdoor pool. One woman shivers and tells me,

"They used to keep it at 85, but had some problems."

Another says I should get weights from a pile by the side of the pool. They are Styrofoam and weigh less than a pound each. Armed, I jump back into the pool to talk health care with the ladies.

The first thing they all agree on is that none carry their Social Security card with them.

"Identity theft,"

explains Gene, one of the youngest, with short blond cropped hair and a huge pale pink hat.

"We wish those numbers weren't printed on our health insurance and Medicare cards, because we use them all the time."

Gene's husband retired from Halliburton, so their Blue Cross/Blue Shield plan is her primary insurance. It's not enough. On top of that, she has Medicare as secondary coverage, as well as supplemental Medicare. Gene is bipolar, suffers massive depression, and has attempted suicide four times. Last July, the FDA approved an implant that her doctors believed would help her. Her insurance company approved the surgery, but not the follow-up care involved. Her Medicare coverage kicks in only when primary stops, not if it doesn't start. This ridiculous catch-22 kept her from getting what she needed.

Cynthia is fair with wire-rim glasses. She doesn't smile much. In the locker room, after our class, she says that her doctor stopped dealing with insurance company policies except Medicare.

"He tells patients if they can't pay bills, he'll work something out. He doesn't want insurance companies telling him how to practice medicine."

When I suggest the possibility of a national plan, her brow wrinkles:

"What, you mean, socialized medicine?"

"Not exactly, but—well, why not?" I ask.

"Because, I like to have a choice in which doctor I go to,"
she answers.

The trouble is that more and more private health insurance policies are not accepted by doctors, who don't have time to deal with all the paperwork they require and restrictions they demand. Plus, employers keep cutting medical benefits for employees and retirees alike. Almost four million Americans lost employer-sponsored health care between 2000 and 2003.[1]

The bottom line is that these women, and the rest of America, can't live without health insurance, which is currently a combination of private companies and government programs. This presents two problems. First, the cost of private insurance is obscene. The Bush solution for that is to encourage people to open "health savings accounts" so they can save the money they don't have for the coverage they can't afford. Second, Bush keeps cutting the public programs that more and more of us are forced to rely on, like Medicare for the elderly and Medicaid for the poor.

A BETTER WAY?

Just after Christmas 2005, I visited Diane Archer, who founded the Medicare Rights Center, in midtown Manhattan. An elderly lady with wild platinum hair, black frames and a slightly hunched back rode the elevator with me. She asked me if I was a volunteer, and I explained that I was writing a book on people's finances and that health care was one chapter. Her response was,

"Help! They sure don't make things easy."

Diane is a slender, intense woman with short black hair and sharp hazel eyes. She gestures with her hands like an Italian mom. She's been trying to launch a Medicare for America idea that resonates, but there are obstacles, even from people like Cynthia who could benefit.

"People have these preconceptions associated with a broader health-care system," she says. "Like 'universal' equals 'communism,' which is un-American. 'Single payer' is too Canada. And 'national health care'—well, that's England; it's not what America is about."

Meanwhile, the number of uninsured Americans has increased each year since Bush took office. It reached a record 46 million in 2005, including 8.4 million children.[2] That doesn't include those with incomplete policies or huge out-of-pocket deductibles and expenses. It does include those who balance the cost of health care with the ability to buy food.

"With private insurance, you're uninsured, underinsured, or anxiously insured,"

says Diane, her fingers flexed to underscore the point. That's an absurdly precarious state for a country as rich as ours.

In April 2005, the House and Senate passed measures that would cut $10 billion from Medicaid over the next five years.[3] The amount was a fraction of the $300 billion annual program, but it made the Republicans feel happy about their ability to balance a budget.

Medicaid provides health care to over 50 million low-income children, pregnant women, senior citizens, and disabled persons.[4] Medicaid supplements the Medicare coverage of 6 million elderly or disabled Medicare beneficiaries. It provides health insurance for a quarter of American children and pays for a third of U.S. births each year. If Bush grasps the financial strains of this country and the high costs of individual health care, he's keeping his wisdom to himself. In his nine-page 2006 State of the Union address, he addressed health care in two whole paragraphs, leading with:

> Keeping America competitive requires affordable health care. Our government has a responsibility to help provide health care for the poor and the elderly, and we are meeting that responsibility.[5]

A few days later, he supported cutting Medicare by $36 billion over the next 5 years and Medicaid by $17.6 billion over 10 years. It is as if he thinks it's a galloping entitlement that he must reign in. He then asked for that $50 billion back to put towards war spending for Iraq and Afghanistan, which his budget director understood to be "a very expensive undertaking."[6]

The thing is, there's this massive wall of money—called $1.7 trillion in projected tax cuts for the wealthy over the next 5 years, or about $3 trillion over the next 10 years—right in front of Bush's face. He could use this money to balance the country's finances and improve the well-being of its citizens. But instead of noticing it, he turns tail and runs miles backwards to pick pennies out of the pockets of the struggling and elderly.

"This administration," says Diane, "has a Darwinian policy—survival of the richest. We could have 125 million uninsured and under this leadership, nothing would change."

Except that it could get worse.

WELCOME TO HOLLYWOOD AND HEALTH CARE

What do a successful ABC television producer, an ex-Los Angeles Laker turned actor, and a former meth addict turned PR god all have in common? First, they all spend way too much time in LA traffic. Second, they all think America's current health-care system sucks.

Poncho Hodges is a 34-year-old former LA Laker. He's the tallest person I've ever stood next to. I walk with him (Poncho used to live in New York, so is down with the whole walking thing) to a nearby Starbucks, on Magnolia and Lankershim Boulevard. My all-black outfit (yes, it *is* a New York thing) looked a little grim next to his red and white Yankee cap and red and white sneakers. His face was framed by bling studs and a thick gold chain necklace.

Poncho attended the University of Colorado on a basketball scholarship. He did a stint as power forward for the Lakers. He's perfectly healthy, now, but having witnessed tons of sports injuries in his career, knows the importance of coverage.

"Health insurance?" he says with a voice as deep as James Earl Jones. "Been winging it."

Like other members in the Screen Actors Guild and various professional groups or unions, he gets insurance through group policies that are imbedded with obstacles.

"I got the SAG one, but, you need to gross like $15,000 a year to keep it. You have to gross about $25,000 to get dental."

For seven years, he played basketball all over Europe, and learned from his time there:

"America needs to take lessons from other countries where if you're a citizen, you get health care, no matter who you are."

Ideas like this separate Poncho from the thinking of our government, even though he considers himself a Republican.

"I like the things they stand for—like on religion—and I'm down with keeping American traditions. On the economic thing, it's different—they don't care about the poor, they're too privileged."

He is further proof that the need for decent health care cuts across political beliefs, and he is one more example of how out of touch conservatives are even with their own constituents.

After Poncho takes off in his size 15 Nikes, I have another latte. For this one I am joined by Jed Wallace, a super-lively PR person. Jed has an expensive individual health insurance plan, which also covers his two young daughters. He got it on-line.

"It's Blue Cross/Blue Shield—over $800 a month, a $10 deductible on office visits, $30 on prescription drugs, $500 on ER work, and an annual deductible of $750."

Part of the reason the plan's so expensive is Jed's former, ultra-Hollywood lifestyle. He craved the dream:

Jacked

"I wasn't exactly sure how, but my ego said I wanted to be rich and famous—then you get pummeled by reality."

Reality for Jed started with smoking pot, than doing hallucinogens. It soon became a full-blown meth addiction. During the mid-'90s, he co-hosted a web radio spot and "Popcorn," a movie review show on MTV. He made, as he put it,

"shitloads of money, burned through it and started doing coke."

MTV was short-lived, so he got into the bar business in Santa Monica.

"It was 'on' from there—partying, drugs, everything."

By April 2000, he was cruising high. The manager of one of the beer companies he bought along the way happened to be his drug dealer.

"I was working 20- to 22-hour days—I had to get into meth, the delusion that with a little, you could do anything."

He rationalized that he provided his 2-year-old and wife a home, money, cars. He paid employees in drugs. Finally, his wife left him. Eventually she returned, and created an intervention that led him to Life's Journey Center in Palm Springs. It was, as he put it,

"a humbling experience. There, we also discovered I was bipolar—that's why my insurance is so high."

Now, he speaks to kids in recovery through Alcoholics Anonymous.

"Lots of people in treatment wind up dead, back on drugs, or in jail. I'm lucky. People helped me. 'Cause it's not covered by insurance."

He's been clean for two years, having been to hell and back, and has met tons of lost people along the way. Many of them, he believes, were souls that could have been helped by wider reaching health care.

"This government is totally detached from the real American psyche and spirit," he says, driving me back to my car. "You parked all the way over here?! Why?"

The next day, I hit ABC Studios, where it was definitely turning Christmas. A young intern was passing out ginger-bread cookies, while I waited for Harry Phillips, a producer of *Primetime*. After a few minutes he arrived, a friendly man with a neatly trimmed gray beard and mustache, and offered me herbal tea from their kitchen.

Behind his desk are several bags of Christmas presents, mostly for his youngest daughter, Abigail.

"She's 12 going on 20,"

he says. On his walls are several Emmy awards, a map of the United States, and a Norman Rockwell print of a young black girl in Mississippi.

He's been at ABC for 16 years. His health plan is through Disney/ABC, and is CIGNA/PPO, for which he pays $250 a month with a $350 annual deductible. Born in Canada on Memorial Day in 1952, he's been in the United States for 15 years but maintains dual citizenship. The biggest reason why? Yep:

"Health care—socialized medicine."

As far as he's concerned, Canada just flat out gives its citizens better care than we do. And it's hard to argue with him. Canada has the equivalent of an interlocking system of Medicare and Medicaid. Everyone's in the same risk pool and there are fewer administrative costs.

His ABC health-care plan is a good one, and Harry knows it. He also realizes how lucky he is compared to many of us: "I'd be willing to give up some of that privilege in return for others to have more access to health care in the U.S." Meanwhile, Harry's holding onto his Canadian national health care (CARE) card and his home in Canada because

"retiring there makes a lot more financial sense."

Sadly, most of us don't have this option. And after all, should we really have to feel "lucky" to have decent health care?

RISING HEALTH-CARE COSTS AND YOUR WALLET

The private health-care system is filled with waste. In 2003, health-care bureaucracy cost the Americans who use it $400 billion.[7] And health insurance companies don't even actually provide *health care*. It's not like GM, which provides cars (or tries to anyway).

Let's make no mistake about this: insurance companies are middlemen. Their sole job is to connect the dots that stand between you and your medical treatment; more often than not, it seems like their job is actually to create red tape between you and your wallet. Why do we put up with them? Because these companies are so entrenched in our daily lives that we can't imagine an alternative. But there are other options, whether or not the Bush conservatives want to acknowledge them. A recent study found that national health insurance, financed by the federal government instead of private insurance companies would save Americans about $286 billion annually in paperwork alone. This would be enough to give all uninsured Americans full prescription drug coverage.[8]

President Bush goes out of his way to ignore these obvious statistics. He goes out of his way to bolster our current system. A system that is only getting worse. Medical expenses rose faster than inflation in the 1990s as insurance companies created plans to limit our treatment options through something they like to call "managed care."[9] To me this translates as: *we* manage our (enormous) profits, *you* wing your (shoddy) coverage.

On top of that, the costs of plans have increased. Between 2000 and 2005, average monthly premiums for individual coverage shot from $342 to $603, and annual deductibles (the amount you put out before your insurance kicks in) almost doubled, to $323 from $175.[10]

To make sure drugs companies weren't left behind as health insurance companies grabbed their enormous profits, the Bush Republicans introduced the prescription drug bill —or "Medicare Part D"—for Medicare beneficiaries, the 42 million Americans who are disabled or 65 or older.[11] In far from conservative wisdom, the bill doesn't include the ability to bargain with drug companies for lower cost drugs. Since its inception, drug companies have substantially raised prices on nearly all drugs covered by the program.[12] Plus, the cost of this drug-company orgy to our federal budget is projected to be a staggering $8.7 trillion between now and 2080.[13] The Medicare prescription drug bill was part of the 2003 Medicare law and took effect in January 2006. Your first $250 of drugs is free. Then comes the cloud, looming behind that slim silver lining: you pay a quarter of costs from $251 to $2,250, and *all* of the next $2,850. That "doughnut hole" lasts until you hit $5,100 in drug costs per year.[14] After that, Medicare picks up most of the tab. All in all, the gap in coverage has only increased with the new plan, and with it, out-of-pocket expenses for the average participant. By January 2006, less than half of the elderly able to sign up for the prescription drug plan did. Why? The sign-up process was nearly impossible to figure out.

> *"The Bush administration knew that going in," Diane Archer told me. "They banked on it. They didn't even keep the right to negotiate prices with the drug companies."*
>
> *"Others who did sign up didn't get their plastic ID cards that confirmed they had, so they couldn't get the drugs they needed,"* she added.

And the problems aren't limited to the people who need those drugs. Before the bill, Medicare's overhead was only 4 percent of its total cost to the federal budget. After the prescription plan was adopted, overhead tripled.[15] Nevertheless, Bush has decided the program is a raging success.[16]

Unfortunately, Bush is not alone. Drug and health insurance companies felt the love that average citizens didn't feel, as they were second only to oil companies in 2005 stock market performance.[17] Once again, those companies book the profits, and we Americans foot the ever-growing bill.

SEATTLE'S UNDERINSURED GENIUS CHILDREN

Port Townsend in northern Washington state is a town of 10,000 people, a place where hippies, retirees, and rednecks co-exist comfortably. After a ferry ride and a three-hour drive from Seattle, I arrive at the home of Dena Shunra. Her place is a modest hodgepodge of books, cats, and computers. Dena's one of the world's foremost English-Hebrew translators, work she does out of her home. A natural caregiver, she has prepared tomato soup (from real tomatoes!) and a fabulous salad.

She has two adorable kids, 7-year-old Rose and 14-year-old Shachaf, both of whom have forms of autism. Shachaf has a 180 IQ and bouts of severe depression. They are both beautiful. Neither child can communicate with other children their age. Her insurance needs are constant and much of their treatment lies outside normal coverage. She has an HSA (health savings account, sort of like the kind that Bush goes on about). But it doesn't exactly make things easier, as it's connected to a local health insurance company plan that costs her $284 a month and has an astoundingly high annual deductible of $5,100.

Her package also doesn't include mental health coverage for her children, which she pays out of pocket. The situation is maddening. She believes that

> *"health care should not be a for-profit thing, period. Like the post office, like roads. Part of what insurance has made happen is you stop seeing doctors and see physician assistants. Then, there are the lab tests."*

She just got a $585 bill for blood tests, which are necessary to decide whether to give her son antidepressants or not.

She spends several hours a day just balancing the family's finances and figuring out how to stretch them for her children's treatment; This, she quips,

> *"is valuable time that could be spent knitting."*

Then she turns serious:

> *"What happened to the Hippocratic oath?" she asks, shaking her head. "It's been hijacked by corporations. Women then get the burden of our faulty health-care system; we are the true caretakers of America."*

DESTITUTE, BUT DETERMINED

Joy Kal lives in New York City. The chapters of her life are divided by her health condition. Now 50, she's gone from fully employed and insured to destitute on Medicaid.

It began well. Intelligent with a passion for medicine, she worked as an emergency medical technician from the ages of 15 through 25. She went to college in 1988 and later enrolled in pre-med courses. She worked as a massage therapist for a number of years.

> *"Then," she says, "I was struck by lower back pain, which doctors determined was caused by herniated discs."*

This turned out to be the wrong prognosis. Between 1988 and 1998, she lost her private insurance, her doctor, and then her apartment. During these years, the specter of AIDS loomed large:

> *"Third-year residents would tell me I was bleeding from some HIV-related disease and dismiss me."*

She couldn't move through the debilitating pain.

> *"You get so demoralized," she says.*

Eventually she ended up on welfare in an Upper West Side hotel with mental patients and severe drug abusers.

It took those 10 years of her navigating the Medicaid system to diagnose a tumor in her uterus. She found a Medicaid doctor willing to operate, only to suffer cerebral asthenia during the procedure; her blood pressure became dangerously low as her brain was deprived of oxygen.

> *"And, here I am, intelligent, white, native English speaker. Imagine others without as many tools going through this."*

After that procedure, her pain was partially relieved, but didn't disappear. Between 1998 and 2000, she approached gynecologists at six different hospitals about the possibility of her having endometriosis. Finally, she found a doctor at Mount Sinai who diagnosed her successfully. It was stage five: the stage it can settle in your kidney and kill you.

> *"My white middle-class friends tried to get their doctors to operate, none would. They laughed—they weren't gonna get paid, so weren't gonna do it."*

Eventually, she was able to get treatment by bartering. A social worker friend referred a client to her: an ADHD sufferer who was studying to become a certified anesthesiologist. Joy coached him through his written and oral exams. This man's wife was a gynecologist, and made a phone call on Joy's behalf to a renowned endometriosis doctor.

Living through the experience made Joy a fighter. She is now a consumer advocate and serves on the board of Physicians for a National Health Program.[18]

Jacked

"When I tell my story," she says over coffee at a Chelsea diner, "I'm illustrating the loss of potential and the need for a better system, like in Canada."

"Medical care is a right, not a privilege," Joy declares, running a finger through her short white hair. "It's shortsighted for the government not to cover basic medical needs. No system is perfect. But, this is America. If we pay attention to the health system, we can outpace the world in quality and care."

6

Your Social Security Card and Keeping the Faith

If you're like me, you've been awed by the sheer amount of "stuff" your grandmothers have accumulated. Old pictures in heavy fake gold frames. Delicate china handed down through the generations. Vintage costume jewelry that now sells for way too much money on eBay. Items with detail and character that all tell stories.

When I entered Maria Vargas' tiny one-bedroom apartment, loaded with memories, I couldn't help but think of my own grandmothers, now deceased. Classical music fills the air. Family photos, antique dolls, and embroidered pillows personalize the living room, making it cozy. A number of American flags complete the decor.

Now in her 90s, Maria lives in a subsidized housing complex in northern Philadelphia called Overmont House. In the midst of an otherwise bleak atmosphere, you enter her unit and step back in time and place. Her knickknacks are like the ones so many of our grandmothers brought from their home countries when they came to live the American dream.

Her daughter, Jenny, lives with her. She is a full-figured woman, wearing brown glasses, hanging earrings, and a flower sweater. Her hair is salt and pepper. Jenny shows me a black and white photo of her mother at the age of 5, as a little girl in Bogotá, Colombia.

Maria and I speak together with the help of Mayra Palencia, a translator and the Hispanic representative for the Center for Advocacy for the Rights and Interests of the Elderly (CARIE), a nonprofit advocacy and action group. For eight years, she's worked with various Hispanic communities in Philly. They used to be mostly Puerto Rican and Caribbean, but now include many Central and South Americans. Maria was referred to Mayra about six years ago, after returning from an extended stay in Colombia and discovering she wasn't receiving Social Security checks for the right amount.

Maria was born in 1914. She met her husband, Narciso, at "chocolate time." Like English tea time or American coffee breaks, Maria would sit around with friends drinking hot chocolate and eating cookies. One day, Narciso joined them.

"It was love at first sight,"

she giggles, after all these years. He wouldn't leave her alone. A mechanic, with strong hands and movie-star looks, he had served in the Colombian army. Maria was dating someone else, but dumped him for Narciso. The two were married a year later, in April 1938.

In one of the pictures on the wall there's a man who looks just like Narciso. It's Jenny's son, David, in army attire. Taking after his grandfather, he served in the U.S. military for eight years and is now a police officer in Philly.

Maria is a tiny woman, maybe 4′10″. Her husband used to call her his "tesorita," or little treasure. Her eyes are sharp and alert as she talks about him. She's wearing black pants and shoes without socks. Draped around her delicate shoulders is a lavender knit sweater with olive, orange, and cream flowers. Her white hair is thick.

In 1970, Narciso was contracted while in Colombia to work in Philly as a diesel motor mechanic on large construction trucks and forklifts. Maria came too, much later, in 1985. Until that time, he sent money back home to her and the family in Bogotá. He was a hard worker and only stopped when he had a minor heart attack. He was 72. After that, Social Security disability became the couple's only income. When Narciso died in 1995, he and Maria had been married 57 years.

"He died in Bogotá, while I was in America,"

says Maria, a teardrop forming in her left eye.

Mother and daughter sit close on the couch, holding hands. Jenny takes over:

> *"We went to the Social Security office with his death certificate, to see if the benefits could be changed to survivor's benefits. The man at the counter said, 'You've lived off the government long enough, be happy with what you got.'"*

Despite this man being a jerk, Maria continued to get disability until 1999. Then she went to the office to report that she was leaving for an extended vacation to Colombia and asked if her check be mailed there. She was told that because she was leaving the country and Colombia had a lower standard of living, she'd get less money. Her benefit dropped from $500 to $350. While in Columbia she contracted bronchitis and had to stay longer than planned.

When she returned to America she asked if her benefit could be moved back up to $500. Jenny, her son David, and Maria went to the Social Security office and found themselves in front of the same man as before. Maria becomes animated as she says that he's been there

"para siempre!" (forever).

With Maria standing there, and David showing him her stamped passport, the man behind the counter refused to acknowledge her. She's short, but not that short. At first, he wouldn't transfer even the $350 back to her Philly address.

The three returned the next day; same guy. He finally decided to notice Maria was standing there, but wouldn't change the amount back to $500. He said her grandson was obligated to keep her. David replied indignantly,

"These benefits are the ones my grandfather worked for."

And this, beautifully summarized, is the point of the Social Security system. It's not a handout, it's an insurance contract protected by the federal government. The premiums you pay come out of your or your spouse's paycheck. The amount you receive is related to what you've contributed over a lifetime of work. The private accounts that Bush talks about simply cannot offer that level of security.

Ultimately, CARIE helped Maria reinstate the $500 rate and get a retroactive payment of $1,700 to make up for the earlier incorrect amounts. Maria now receives $603 a month, adjusted for inflation. The apartment costs $366 a month, a third of what Maria and Jenny, who worked for 15 years as an office cleaner and is on her own monthly disability of $622, receive together. Their rent includes electricity and gas. They pay for food, phone, cable, clothing, and Boomer, their gray cat. They're thankful for what they get; they've made a home with it.

> *"I don't think private accounts are a very good idea," says Jenny, "They come with no guarantee that it'll be there when you retire. I don't want any handouts; I just want to know that I'll get what I need based on what I put in."*

Jenny offers strong coffee and butter cookies, served on a silver platter covered with a white lace towel. I ask whether either of them has ever invested in the stock market. Mayra translates and they both burst out laughing. I take that as a "no." They are both registered as Independents but voted for Clinton, Gore, and Kerry.

> *"I don't agree with Bush's policies on anything," says Jenny. "When Clinton became president, the country was in crisis and he stabilized it. Bush came and collapsed it."*

SOCIAL SECURITY AND BEN FRANKLIN

Not far away from Maria's home is Independence Hall, where the Declaration of Independence was signed in 1776. At the time, Benjamin Franklin said,

> *"We must all hang together, or assuredly we shall all hang separately."*[1]

Ben got it. America, a magnet for the poor, persecuted, and proud, was built on this premise—strength comes from community.

About a century and a half later, our Social Security system was built on the same premise. When Social Security was created in 1935 by Franklin Delano Roosevelt as part of the New Deal (the operative word being *deal*), the government couldn't pretend the country was doing better than it was. The evidence to the contrary was everywhere, jumping out of windows and standing in soup lines that circled entire neighborhoods. Having citizens pay into a system that safeguarded their money until they retired or became disabled was a way for the government to stabilize the country. Such logic seems too old school and quaint for Bush's conservatives; they prefer raiding this money over using it to insure our country.

Privatizing Social Security was a key part of the Republican platform in the 2000 election. Essentially, Bush sought to replace the foundation of the program—the government's guarantee of your money for your future—with the creation of individual "private accounts" that people would maintain with the help of all those honest Wall Street brokers. The idea was shelved after the stock market bubble burst in 2001, wiping out trillions of dollars and big chunks of people's non-Social Security retirement savings.

Amazingly, the idea was resurrected in 2003, once the market recovered enough to make the Bush administration assume people had forgotten about the risks. Democrats, progressive groups, a few visionary Republicans, and a lot of ordinary Americans, especially older voters, openly disagreed with him. W. eventually realized that taking a swipe at all the elderly in America was a bad idea, or at least the timing wasn't great. So, after two years of trying to convince everyone—probably even his mother—that the Social Security system would go the way of eight-track cartridges and black and white TVs any second, he slowed down his relentless scare tactics about the system being broken.

But his silence was temporary. Because somewhere beneath the surface was a group of people (the Bush conservatives, to be exact) content to watch the system die and make everyone pay their own damn way when they get old. Their logic? That there aren't enough young people to support all the older ones that keep living so long. The translation: baby boomers aren't doing their part for the American economy and Social Security by dying off quickly enough.

Not all of us in this country are up on the details of its history, but you'd think that President Bush and his friends would at least remember the last couple decades. When the Social Security Act was signed in 1935, the tax rate—the percentage of an employees' salary that went into the Social Security Trust Fund—was set at 2 percent. Over the next 65 years, the rate gradually increased to make up for the growing elderly population.

In 1983, President Ronald Reagan asked Alan Greenspan (just before Greenspan became the chairman of the Federal Reserve) to study problems that might be caused by aging baby boomers, those born from the mid-1940s to early 1960s. To assure that Social Security would have enough money when these boomers hit retirement age, Greenspan's commission raised the tax rate from 8.05 percent to its current 12.4 percent. Thanks to this change, the Social Security Trust Fund accumulated a $1.7 trillion surplus over the next 20 years. Enough to cover the boomer generation.

So what's Bush ranting and raving about? More baby boomers didn't magically appear between 1983 and 2003, when Bush decided to attack their longevity. The problem, that his conservatives don't want to address, is that a hell of a lot of this extra money has been "borrowed" by the government, to support their extravagant spending habits (read: the military, tax cuts for the rich, and debt payments). By the end of 2004, the $1.7 trillion surplus had diminished to $153 billion.[2]

STRENGTH IN STRUGGLING

The next day, I went with Diane Menio, the executive president of CARIE, to visit Mattie Brown. Mattie was born on Second Street, the borderline of Delaware County, in 1940. Mattie is part Jewish, part African-American, part Seneca Indian, but most importantly, she is a trip. She's wearing a purple sweatsuit, talks a mile a minute, and gets around town on a scooter that she keeps in her apartment. As a child, she was often ill. She was born with arthritis and a rheumatic heart.

"Now," she says, "the only thing not wrong with me is my kidney and liver."

When she met Franklin Brown, her second husband, she was a licensed beautician and cosmetologist. The two eventually split, but never divorced. He died on May 10, 2005. She found out through a letter from Social Security.

"It was a real shock," she says. "I was still getting over my mother's death."

Mattie started getting his survivors benefit of $948 a month in August 2005, but it's still a struggle to make ends meet.

"I'm overdrawn already," she says, four days into March. "It's hard when you gotta pay for food, transportation, and co-pay."

Mattie has to shell out a co-pay of $3 to $5 every time she buys drugs. She takes 25 different pills a day and she's on oxygen at night.

Mattie lives in a one-room studio, divided into a kitchen and bedroom area. Her little couch is covered with patchwork dolls and teddy bears. On the kitchen table is a canister of sugar, empty mugs, KOOL cigarettes

("it's my only vice," she says),

bills, and many bottles of pills. She points to her bed, on which is a new light blue comforter, then to her new curtain rods, because the old ones broke, then to faux lace curtains, because the old ones had holes.

"I did it,"

she says each time. Her pride is evident, in spite of her difficulties:

"This morning I paid $35 dollars on an overdrawn check to my bank, PNC. But, no sense in raising hell about it, 'cause I did it."

I ask her about her DVD player, which stands out amidst the bare furnishings.

"I was at Radio Shack and told the lady that I had $40.08 in the bank. She got me a $300 credit card," Mattie says. "When I lost my home, I couldn't get banks to help me, and here I got credit in 10 minutes."

I examine the glossy Radio Shack AnswersPlus Card, issued by credit card giant Citibank USA, N.A. That's retail America for you—they'll charge 30 percent interest on a card you don't need and give you a credit limit you can't afford and will probably never be able to pay off. It's so very "conservative."

I ask Mattie what she thinks of Bush's moves to change Social Security into a private account system. She answers,

> *"My skin might be brown, and I might be old, but I'm not stupid. If Bush changes things over, you'll be looking for your own drawers."*

I ask her what she'd do if she were elected president.

> *"If it was up to me, it wouldn't be just up to me, it'd be up to the people. I'd put medicine back where it was and make it better for poor folks. Anyone making over 50 or 60K can make co-payments. We can't. We live hand-to-mouth."*

It must be noted that no one I spoke with talked about Social Security without trashing Bush's Medicare Prescription Plan D, a.k.a. the drug company handout plan. It is a program that has single-handedly confused and gouged nearly every senior in the country.

SOCIAL SECURITY HELPS EVERYONE

There are people like Maria and Mattie who depend on Social Security to live, and others who rely on it to supplement their retirement. Their perspectives and life circumstances may be different, but they all stress its importance as a guaranteed source of income. Don and Diane Factor live outside Philly, in a suburb called Dresher. They are both semi-retired, but work part time. They keep finishing each other sentences when they speak with me.

Diane is 65, and just began collecting Social Security. Diane teaches art part time at a nonprofit arts center. She's been doing it for 30 years:

> *"My hair is white, but I still love kids, so I'm a little bit crazy."*

Don also gets a small amount. He worked for the Department of Defense as a logistics manager for the Marines, and helped on navy aircrafts for years. While there, he did have money withheld for Social Security but it was funneled into his army pension. As with many workers in other fields, this means he receives his military pension but only gets a bit of Social Security money, from work done outside the army. To supplement he does taxes for middle-income folks at H&R Block.

Diane and Don know that the system is in danger.

> *"Social Security has been utilized and depleted," says Diane. "It's not sacrosanct to my knowledge."*

> *"Look at IBM," adds Don, at the same time. "It's now freezing pensions. Some people may feel they're astute, but the older you are, the more dependent you are on people giving you advice. Those brokers are particularly terrible with old people. And what do you do when a year like 2001 comes again?"*

He never agreed with the idea that people should invest in their own accounts.

> *"The vast majority of people don't know what they're doing," he says. "With Social Security, you don't have to understand anything, you just get it."*

"Think about Enron and people in their 60s and 70s who need to go back to work just to survive. Social Security was the one thing you could rely on," replies Diane.

"Social Security is a mainstay for people who get anything from $1,000 to $1,500 a month, and the spouse who gets half. Together it's sa good amount. You can't retire on it, but it's a good system," adds Don.

Diane cuts in, "We're in the minority of the population. We don't rely on it for food and lodging—still, I like my Social Security—I paid into it." Don and Diane could do without Social Security if they had, too, but it certainly helps them. They also understand the importance of Social Security for all Americans, poor, middle class, and even the rich.

SECURING SOCIAL SECURITY

Does Social Security have some problems? Yes, but estimates show that they won't become an issue for another 35 years.[3] Are people living longer? Yes. Today, 12 percent of the population is over 65. The trustees of Social Security in Washington say that number will be 18 percent in 20 years, 21 percent in 45 years, and 23 percent in 75 years.[4] Clearly, we need to deal responsibly with this growth.

But is Bush's vision a responsible one? In a word, no. If Bush—or his conservatives who remain in government after his second term ends—get their wish, Americans will be totally on the hook for their retirement (because companies sure as hell won't be). The damage will be huge, both to individuals and to the government. According to one estimate, just to make up for the money diverted away from Social

Security and into private accounts will cost the federal budget $4.5 trillion over the next two decades.[5]

And beyond these terrifying statistics, Bush's argument—that the stock market is a great place for people to invest their retirement—is just plain stupid. Ask the people who invested 401(k) retirement funds in Enron stock as it tanked. Plus, the idea of individual investment has Wall Street salivating; they're already searching for ways to eke out extra commissions from your retirement pot.

Besides, how can Bush keep exclaiming about the virtues of an "ownership society"'—in which each citizen is responsible for their own future—while his government recklessly overspends. The logic just isn't there. So he's resorted, once again, to scaring people into believing that the Social Security program will disappear, so they need to create individual accounts. Carl Malfitano, Retiree Chairperson, UAW Region 1, put it best: "It's like Colonel Sanders telling the chickens he's there to save them."[6]

A responsible government should find ways to keep promises to its citizens that don't involve screwing their future security. $3.7 trillion—the amount Social Security's trustees recently cited as a likely shortfall over the next 75 years—is a fraction per year (think 6 cents out of $100) of the debt that the country owes *now*. Call me crazy—it seems to me more important to take care of our debt today. But if our government were to address this issue more seriously, Bush and company would have to acknowledge their horrific habit of spending money the country doesn't have. Since taking office, the Bush administration has "borrowed" $700 billion from the Social Security Trust Fund, in addition to all the other debts they've been piling onto the country.[7]

Privatizing Social Security would put more American seniors below the poverty line. In particular, women (who earn on average three quarters of what men earn) and minorities, like Maria and Mattie, would see their situations deteriorate, since their life expectancy is longer.[8] As it stands, 78 percent of seniors between the ages of 65 and 80 (and 11.6 percent over age 85) depend on Social Security to live. Approximately half of seniors rely on Social Security to stay out of poverty.[9] This includes survivors, who are mostly women, receiving benefits of deceased relatives. Bush's individual accounts won't provide the disability and survivor benefits that the current system offers and that so many rely on.

But let's give Bush the benefit of the doubt for a moment. Let's assume he is really concerned and sincerely wants to help out. Do you know how easily he could do this? How easily he could make himself a hero to the average American? For one, he could have considered raising payroll taxes. Instead, at the end of 2004, he decided against this idea without any real explanation.[10] Likewise, he could consider rolling back tax cuts on the wealthy. His tax cuts alone will cost at least *five* times as much as any potential Social Security shortfall over the next 75 years. Or put another way, taking back just one-third of these cuts would shore up Social Security for a century.[11] But while his conservative cronies hold sway, we shouldn't count on our president—or any similar successor—acting responsibly towards the vast majority of Americans.

Instead of dismantling one of the only American systems that has consistently worked, focusing on ways to secure it might be—well—more social. There are three solutions: 1) stop raiding the Social Security Trust Fund for unrelated purposes, 2) raise the cap so rich people pay more proportional Social Security tax, or 3) stop letting people live so long. This third option definitely isn't more "social," let alone legal. But despite what your government tells you, the first two options are totally viable.

For instance, those who earn more money could pay more Social Security tax. The way the system stands, people who earn millions or $90,000 are taxed the *same* amount—Bill Gates, Donald Trump, President Bush. People earning less than $90,000 get taxed on *all* their earnings, and people making more, don't.[12] If Congress moved the cap up to include all the earnings of all Americans, they would—just like that—have $100 billion more in the Social Security pot each year.[13] Once we secure these funds, we as a people should demand our president not spend them on anything but our Social Security needs. Bush and his fellow conservatives are like kids around a cookie jar: their hands reach in again and again.

Above all, we've got to keep our eyes open. Just, for example, when we thought the issue of attacking Social Security was behind us, Bush's agenda rose from the molten ash like the Terminator. In his 2007 budget he suggested a plan to let people set up private accounts by 2010. This plan means that $700 billion would leave the Social Security system and go into private accounts over the following seven years.[14] We, the American people, cannot afford this.

In his 2006 State of the Union address, he asked Congress to join him in "creating a commission to examine the full impact of baby boomer retirees on Social Security, Medicare, and Medicaid."[15] *But George, we did that.* In 1983. Why he keeps suggesting more layers of government to do what existing layers are already doing (or have already done two decades ago) is a mystery. Yet, like the Department of Homeland Security, which was created despite having a Defense Department (which we all assumed protects the homeland), he suggested a new commission to do work that's already being done. In other words, he wastes taxpayer money looking into programs that work so he can stop the benefits they provide.

Let's get this straight: Social Security is not an investment scheme. It's not a free handout. It's a vital American institution. Social Security is a promise to America, paid for by Americans, and it should be respected and preserved as such.

FARMERS

DECLARATIONS
HOMEOWNERS
Replaces all prior Declarations, if any

PROTECTOR PLUS
FIRE INSURANCE EXCHANGE

TRANSACTION TYPE: OFFER OF RENEWAL at described residence premises.
The Policy Period is effective (not prior to time applied for)

POLICY PERIOD
ISSUING OFFICE:
ANYTOWN USA

POLICY NUMBER | FROM: 05-05-2006 | TO: 05-05-2007
55555-55-555

This policy will continue for successive policy periods.

INSURED'S NAME & MAILING ADDRESS: LOCATION OR DESCRIPTION OF RESIDENCE PREMISES:
(Same as mailing address unless otherwise stated.)

JOHN Q. PUBLIC & JANE Q. PUBLIC
5555 5TH AVE
ANYTOWN US
55555-5555

7

Your Home Insurance Policy and True Homeland Security

You can get some kick-ass breakfast in the South. Like the one in Fairhope, Alabama, that I shared at Bill and Becky's inn with three teachers who escaped Pascagoula, Mississippi, for the weekend. Our morning meal consisted of homemade grits, a plate of bananas, strawberries and Asian pears smothered in brown sugar, scrambled eggs, warm biscuits, fresh coffee and orange juice, and a substantial helping of King Cake—a pre–Mardi Gras specialty of cream and chocolate decorated with a tiny silver baby on top.

These teachers call their 57,000-person town the "forgotten city."

They range in age from their 50s to early 60s. The eldest, Lynn Duncan, is lovely, with crystal blue eyes, carefully applied makeup, and striking silver hair gathered in a neat bun. She has been living in the top floor of her home since Hurricane Katrina; the bottom floor is uninhabitable.

*"About 85 percent of our town took on water; we didn't stay,"
says Lynn. "I went to Jackson, but my next-door neighbor
stayed. He saw his wife and children off and said he needed
to protect his property. Turned out there was nothing left to
protect."*

Everyone, it seems, has a similar horror story. Linda Wiggens, a gregarious and articulate woman with short curly blond hair, gray eyes, and wire rim glasses, is eager to share hers:

*"We live on the beach, along with more than 75 houses, about
110 to 115 years old. They're 'gone to the slab.'"*

She motions her hand to show that these houses have been flattened down to their foundations.

*"After four months, the house next to mine is the same as it
was then. I feel like I'm living in a garbage dump. Waveland
and Bay St. Louis are gone—they have to start over," says
Linda. "We have a different problem—we need to work from
what we have."*

Sadly, the tragedy of Hurricane Katrina is no longer restricted to its physical destruction. A new horror is unfolding, involving exactly those who are supposed to come to the aid of the destitute: insurance companies. These insurers, like State Farm, Allstate, and Nationwide, are debating whether the tremendous damage was caused by wind (which they cover) or water (which they don't). This has not been a happy situation for people on the Gulf Coast. In Ocean Springs,

Mississippi, spray-painted on one ransacked house, are the words that say it all: *You think Katrina was bad, wait until you meet my Allstate agent.*

Linda says,

"Adjusters have been around looking at houses. They say that damage is from water, not wind. My neighbor had $350K of structure insurance. They gave him $30K."

Our host, Becky, nods as she serves more biscuits.

"In Fairhope, we were inundated with adjusters."

The teachers are intrigued:

"What did they talk about around the breakfast table?"

Becky replies,

"They say that it's old damage that people are trying to push off as new."

(Sure, 30-foot waves blown in by 175-mile-per-hour winds. Old damage.) Amazingly, this is what people all over the Gulf Coast are having to deal with.

In an interesting turn of events, Mississippi's Republican Senator Trent Lott is one of those people. He had a house in front of Lynn's; it was leveled by the storm. In October 2005, he added an inclusion to an existing Senate bill. It allowed Katrina victims not originally covered for floods under the federal flood program to be covered by the federal government after the fact, as if they had been in the program all along.[1] (Since Hurricane Camille in 1969, the federal government has been subsidizing private flood insurance under the

National Flood Insurance Program.) Not only did Lott jump to action in the Senate with uncharacteristic populist generosity, but, like a true progressive hero, he personally took on the insurance companies. In mid-December 2005, Lott's brother-in-law, famed Mississippi attorney Richard "Dickie" Scruggs, filed a federal suit on behalf of him and his wife, Tricia, against Lott's insurance company, State Farm.[2]

Scruggs, who helped win the 48-state, $250 billion settlement against big tobacco companies—immortalized in the hit 1999 film *The Insider,* starring Al Pacino and Russell Crowe—had a nearby beachfront home of his own gutted.[3] Which meant that this time it was personal for the liberal litigator. Said Scruggs,

> *"This is the first time I'm involved in a suit that's affected people I've known all my life. It essentially wiped them out . . . somebody's got to do this."*[4]

The suit revolves around the question of whether a wind-driven water surge should be considered a flood; the companies say they shouldn't have to pay claims to people who didn't have flood policies for which the insurance companies could be liable. Nationwide, Allstate, State Farm, and other insurance companies claim their policies exclude flooding caused by storm surges. Scruggs argues that people were led to believe otherwise. And really, if you lived near a hurricane zone, why would you get a policy that *doesn't* offer protection in a hurricane?

Lott said he was filing the claim because his longtime insurance company

> *"will not honor my policy, nor those of thousands of other South Mississippians, for coverage against wind damage due to Hurricane Katrina."*[5]

This made Lott more of a folk hero in his state than anything else he has ever done. Everyone I spoke with mentioned the suit, and how, in their minds, he was fighting for them.

Insurance companies fear that if Scruggs wins any of the 4,000 individual suits he's filed, on behalf of all the people facing similar situations, it would cost the industry tens of billions of dollars.[6] I have a hard time feeling pity for these companies. Maybe they should have thought about the possibility of paying out on claims when they decided to be property and casualty insurance companies. That is, after all, their job.

ACE AND FEMA

Near Lott's destroyed home, cranes attached to two gigantic GMC trucks are scooping up debris. As they lift junk from piles three people high, workers spray water to keep the dust down. An auditor from the Army Corp of Engineers (ACE) is watching over them.

> *"We've made a lot of progress," he tells me, wishing not to be identified. "We have a full plate."*

These workers are from one of the seemingly countless contractors that have been assigned different cleanup tasks. Contractors tend to get paid upfront by the federal government through ACE or FEMA—unlike, say, most of the inhabitants of the area, who have to fill out tons of forms and then wait for their money.

As I watch the contractors in action, the auditor says,

> *"I make sure we're getting the biggest bang for the buck."*

The "we" he's referring to are the taxpayers. The trucks have white placards on their sides with two numbers on them; one is an identification number, the other is the cubic yards of debris that the truck can hold. The truck in front of me is numbered 115125 and 25. "We" pay contractors by the truckload. I ask why the trucks aren't being filled to their cut-off mark. The auditor tells me this is common with material that doesn't pack as neatly as sand or water. Meaning it's possible for contractors to fill up 10 cubic yards, but charge for 25. (I'm just saying.) Two roads down, I pass a series of wrecked homes with FEMA trailers in their driveways. Then I come to a huge parking lot; it is filled with rows of empty trailers standing there doing nothing. The woman on watch tells me that I can't enter without a permit.

Bush addressed Gulf reconstruction efforts—in the *American* Gulf, that is—with two whole paragraphs of his nine-page 2006 State of the Union speech. (Iraq's reconstruction efforts got two pages.) He said:

> So far, the federal government has committed $85 billion for the people of the Gulf Coast and New Orleans. We're removing debris and repairing highways and rebuilding stronger levees. We're providing business loans and housing assistance. . . .
>
> In New Orleans, and in other places, many of our fellow citizens have felt excluded from the promise of our country. . . . As we recover from a disaster, let us also work for the day when all Americans are protected by justice, equal in hope and rich in opportunity.[7]

Yes, Mr. President. Except that only $18.5 billion was marked for helping people in the American Gulf rebuild their homes. Halliburton, alone, got $11 billion for reconstruction projects in the Middle East.[8]

As for business loans—well, by the end of 2005, the Small Business Administration (SBA), which runs disaster recovery programs for the federal government, had managed to process only a *third* of the loan applications it received. It rejected 82 percent of the ones that it did process.[9] According to the SBA, that's because these applications *needed* to be rejected, so the applicants could be eligible for FEMA grants. FEMA, apparently not getting the message, referred two million people to the SBA for loans. All that red tape is challenging. And more than a little maddening.

And Mr. President, in the midst of all this need, and on top of an already hefty defense budget, Iraq and Afghanistan got an extra $320 billion during the first three years of war.[10] In the beginning of February 2006, your administration requested *another* $120 billion for the Middle East and just $18 billion for hurricane relief in our *American* Gulf.[11] Not exactly the kind of national priorities that help our nation where it needs it the most.

CASINOS AND INSURANCE COMPANIES IN BILOXI

After checking out the FEMA trailers, I take a drive along Beach Boulevard in Biloxi, heading west with Rex and Beth Yeisley.

> *"The town had just started to come back after Camille," says Rex, who moved here in the mid-1990s with his wife, Beth, to become chief financial officer of the Isle of Capri Casinos, Inc. "Never fully, and it took a long time, but in recent years— the casinos were bringing about a better local economy."*

The devastation on the Mississippi coast is humbling. The limited media coverage it got in the wake of Katrina, relative to New Orleans, doesn't prepare you for the 70-mile ride west on Highway 90, where along the beach there is little left of the hundreds of tourist shops, gas stations, and piers.

Across from the Isle of Capri Casino and Hotel is a huge building that I thought was a destroyed parking garage. On closer inspection it turns out to be the Grand Casino, a 100,000-square-foot barge. Katrina's surge picked it up, carried it across the road, and dumped it on top of another building. There's a sad sign on it now: *Grand Casino, Rest in Pieces.*

Next to it is the Old Lady Luck Barge, which has clearly seen luckier times. The President Casino lies on top of a Holiday Inn, half a mile away from its mooring. The Hard Rock Casino, one of the latest additions to the beachfront businesses, never opened. It was constructed with money raised through junk bonds. Bond holders and insurance companies are now fighting over who gets paid and who pays out. The only unharmed bit is the giant guitar.

As we continue this morbid tour, Rex says,

"It'll take five, ten years to recover everything."

House after house has been demolished. December 19, 2005 —three and a half months after Katrina hit—was the first time nonresidents were allowed down the road. Signs on these broken homes aren't all friendly: *We are home—will shoot.* The Mississippi coastline gets worse heading toward New Orleans. A string of what once were souvenir shops are gone, and gas stations are leveled except for a few Shell and Exxon billboards that jut uselessly from the bleak landscape.

"It looks like a bomb went off," sighs Beth.

The lovely old Treasure Bay Boat has been destroyed. In front of Beauvoir, former Confederate President Jefferson

Davis' home, a sign promises the house will be rebuilt. Next door is a shattered home with a less optimistic sign: *You loot—We shoot.* Many of these homes were above the previous high water mark set by Camille, so the owners never took out flood insurance.

We pass by a totaled McDonald's, IHOP, Denny's, Waffle House, and Olive Garden. You name it, it's gone. Firehouses and funeral homes are gutted. The 155th National Guard Unit, in Iraq for a year, will have few jobs when they return. Two VA hospitals are decimated, as well as a senior citizens home. Left behind are slabs. The pictures that the Air Force took days after Katrina resemble almost exactly the landscape five months later. Rex estimates that it'll take almost $200 billion just to rebuild the Mississippi Gulf Coast—half of what Iraq will cost by the end of 2006.

There are no spots in the vicinity left unscathed. And beyond the property damage is the personal damage that will linger on for years to come. Comments Rex,

> *"People who suffer the most are the least educated and poorest who don't have the wherewithal to get what they need."*

GOD AND BUSH

The next morning, I attended a Sunday mass at Our Lady of Fatima Church, in Biloxi. Father Patrick was gracious, and very Irish, in flowing Kermit-green robes. The churchgoers are an eclectic bunch. As the Father puts it,

> *"we are a diverse parish, of rich, poor, old, young, donut makers and truck drivers, doctors and nurses, teachers and students."*

It has one of area's few bilingual masses. One of his prayers extends to the military in Iraq—

"may their efforts lead to lasting peace."

Katrina is neither out of sight nor mind. During his sermon, Father Patrick pauses and asks the parish,

"Who was that prophet that went to David?—help me out here—hurricane moment."

I can't help but see his sermon as a message about the difference between who gets helped by insurance companies and who gets screwed. It is about the prophet, Nathan, who went to King David to tell him a story about a rich and a poor man. The rich one had a flock of sheep. The poor one had only one lamb—which he cared for like it was part of his family. The rich man was having a big banquet and wanted a lamb, but not one of his own. So he killed the poor man's lamb, the innocent and gentle one, just to add to his feast. Religious interpretations aside, even though homes of both the rich and the poor along the Gulf Coast were destroyed, it's the rich that have the greater wherewithal to move or to argue with insurance companies.

One of the parishioners, Tricia Harvey, a blond woman with a white sweater whose home was half destroyed by Katrina, says,

"We called FEMA and asked if we could get a trailer; some people just got theirs last week. Some of the money you get from FEMA, like the $5,000 we got, gets you maybe a roof. But we will do what we need to."

Her family couldn't get insurance because of their home's age and the material from which it was built.

> *"We still live in the house," she says. "Well, the part that's still there."*

She sighs and continues:

> *"I wish more congressmen and senators would come down here because I don't think people grasp what happened. It's all about New Orleans. My friend's living in a six by four trailer with her four children. I think it'll be years before things are rebuilt."*

Mary Ford Francis, a woman in her 50s, wears red plastic glasses pushed up over short dark hair and funky gold vintage earrings—a Christmas present that she says has made people stop calling her Sister Mary. She is President of the St. Vincent de Paul Society, a part of Fatima Church that helps parishioners in need. She ran its relief center from September 5 to October 23, 2005, distributing supplies to hurricane victims. Now, the center has returned to its regular roll of finding homes and food. Mortgage companies gave the victims of Hurricane Katrina a four-month grace period on payments, but they still had to pay all that money afterwards.

> *"One lady," says Mary, "had $700 a month in payments and $2,800 to come up with after four months—but she couldn't get a FEMA trailer during that time or live in her house. So she rented a trailer for $500 month. She was a single mom with two teenagers who wound up taking what was left of her salary—after paying for the trailer and setting aside the mortgage payments—to buy sheetrock. She repaired her*

garage herself so they could live there. Her house can
be repaired, but she got no money from insurance."

As we've seen already, if you have homeowners insurance, wind damage is covered, but water damage from rising water isn't. Of course, it's tough to determine what caused the damage if the house has been wiped off the face of the earth. Who can say whether the roof came off because of wind or flood if it's not there?

The insurance companies look at the water line. According to them (and their rather obscurely written policies), everything above that line—i.e., water that could have come from the sky—is covered, and everything below—i.e., water that might have come from the sea—is not. People were told they didn't need flood insurance if they were not in the flood zone established after Hurricane Camille.

"My husband called after Katrina to get flood insurance.
The insurance company said we weren't in a flood zone,
even though Katrina had just ransacked our home," says
Mary.

What has saved the thousands of people devastated by Hurricane Katrina has been each other. In Biloxi, as in so many other places, the initial response of the community was that people moved in with family and friends. In each neighborhood, the homes least damaged received the most people. After that, people were more able to get help from the government, Salvation Army, or the Red Cross. Says Mary,

"A bunch of 18-wheelers with $3.5 million of supplies
arrived, seven weeks after the storm, through the church
network. The churches made it work efficiently—God was
directing it—because the government and all the larger

institutions with all their planning—they couldn't do what we did."

HELPING YOUR NEIGHBORS

I met Scott and Jackie Cooper after mass and visited their home the next day. In a very "small world" kind of way, the couple met in New York City a few blocks from where I live, at the club Limelight, now called Avalon. They live on Paradise Lane in North Biloxi with their three young children, Alyssa, Logan, and Sofia. They consider themselves lucky.

> *"We didn't get devastated," says Jackie, an attractive woman with olive skin and black hair. "We took in our neighbors, Hope and Colin, both doctors, and split our house in half while they waited for a FEMA trailer, which they got after five weeks. Another family lived in a trailer they set up in my front yard. It was 110 degrees and the mosquitoes were thick. We cooked and lived together. We created a mini-commune that extended to sixteen people."*

The Cooper's home is modest. It's cluttered with books, pictures on the refrigerator, and stacks of dishes in the sink. After housing a small army, they got $700 from FEMA. Says Scott:

> *"It was a very annoying situation: FEMA, MEMA [Mississippi Emergency Management Agency], the Salvation Army, Red Cross—they'd come by with free, yet inedible, food. Pots of bean soup. We took it, but the dogs ate it mostly."*

The improvisation required by people's living situations was, sadly, matched by the difficulty of dealing with the FEMA red tape.

Jacked

"You got in lines with security guards on both sides to speak to the FEMA officials," says Scott. "You try to 'play' them, to get the one that's the nicest, that will help you the most. Then, they send you home with a granola bar or something to make you feel better."

He's in his mid-40s, youthful with blue eyes, simultaneously clean-shaven and rugged.

"I'd lost my job," says Jackie.

She was working at an orthopedic clinic, but Popps Ferry Bridge, which connects south and north Biloxi, was totaled

"so I couldn't get to work."

Eventually, Jackie got a job working with elderly that were displaced from the beachfront assisted-living facilities into her nursing facility. The staff had no homes either, after the hurricane,

"so everyone was sleeping where I worked, on mats," she explains.

Scott was a dealer at the Isle of Capri Casino and Hotel and lost his job. While Jackie goes to work, Scott watches his three kids and some neighborhood ones. There are three dogs roaming about, one of which belonged to a neighbor, a black mixed-breed puppy rescued from a nearby Wal-Mart after Katrina. Scott had just become a casino dealer. He was making $20 to $30 an hour,

"but it wasn't for me—I don't like gambling. I became 'Mr. Mom' when my wife went to graduate school."

"We're in a rebuilding process," he says, making me tea. "Insurance is a scam. I say that as a tax-paying citizen. What I can't understand is that in a country as large as ours, where 100,000 people have been devastated, insurance companies are threatening to back out of Mississippi. That's where the President and Congress should step in and say 'NO.'"

Like so many of us, Scott has recently been reminded that the inequalities of this country run deep.

"The people who benefit are the ones who always do, who had the $600,000 insurance policy versus the $100,000 that we had with tons of loopholes you missed because you didn't have the time or training to deal with them."

I consider the two lambs in Father Patrick's sermon. I know that Rex and Beth had to pull strings to get their home fixed, and that others wouldn't even know where to find those strings.

"I have house insurance from Countrywide," says Scott, returning to a sore subject. "We're dictated in this country to have insurance for everything—your life, home, car, property. But, when you need it, they don't come through. We got the runaround, no returned phone calls. My own insurance guy had left town."

Scott never left town. He wrote about his post-Katrina life in a late October 2005 email blast that he sent to "Friends and the Outside World": *We know in the long run victory is our goal and we won't be beaten. Life after Katrina has sharpened our senses and priorities.*

In a speech given during a mid-January visit through the Mississippi coast, Bush continued his long-standing practice of not helping the Americans who most need help. He confirmed that the federal government would *not* be getting in the way of the insurance companies:

> *"I know you got a lawsuit here: I'm not going to talk about the lawsuit."*

Let me make sure I'm not sharing that quote from his speech out of context. Bush said that after joking about an old woman he'd met during an earlier trip to Biloxi:

> *An old lady walked up to me . . . and I said,*
> *"How are you doing?"*
>
> *And she looked at me and she said,*
> *"Not worth a darn."*
>
> *And I said,*
> *"Well I don't blame you."*
>
> *She said,*
> *"I've been paying all my life for my insurance. Every time that bill came I paid it. . . . And, all of a sudden the storm hit, Mr. President, and it came time to collect, and they told me, no."*
>
> *And she was plenty unhappy and she was looking for anybody she could be unhappy with, and I just happened to be the target.*[12]

No, Mr. President, you actually *were* someone she thought might be able to help her, a subtle difference that may have gone above your head.

Insurance companies posted profits for 2005. Despite Katrina and $3 billion of total claims, net income for the industry increased by 4.4 percent, or $29 billion.[13] Not only that, companies promised shareholders and investors that they would raise their disaster premiums substantially in 2006, even though they haven't paid out on a hefty chunk of claims. All the while, they're hoping that Dickie Scruggs doesn't make them the next tobacco industry. My hope is that he does.

8

Beyond Your Wallet

You can learn a lot about people from their wallets. I learned that Port Townsend, Washington, has more library cards per inhabitant than anywhere else in the country. That Wells Fargo has charming scenery on their debit cards. That ATM cards can open *real* doors.

In my travels, I also discovered that identity theft is a big concern. In crowded places, people seem to prefer paying with credit card rather than debit cards, because credit card fraud is less terrifying than someone being able to pluck cash out of your checking account. I also found that coast to coast and everywhere in between, health care seems to be the single most important issue for Americans. People with coverage are worried that their premiums won't stop rising or that an uncovered condition in their family will bankrupt them. Those without private coverage are scared that Medicare or Medicaid won't be enough. Throw Medicare Prescription Plan D in the mix, for which I could find no support *anywhere*, and there's angst about co-pays on the increasingly expensive drugs for which Bush conservatives didn't bother to set price caps (a policy that actually could have saved more American money from the hands of drug companies).

These concerns point to a deeper issue in American life: the challenge of real security—not just the homeland variety, which has its own problems. People who worked in factories after World War II remember when they could put in an honest week's work, get their wages, and afford to support whole families. Like Jerry Fisher, the retired union leader from Pontiac, Michigan, who worked over forty years at GM when it wasn't eliminating pensions and outsourcing jobs to places with national health care and no minimum wages. Jerry carried an entire family on his plant job, with full health-care benefits and a guaranteed pension for life. Now we don't expect anything like that kind of security. Some executives have it, but only the very rich will be able to dodge financial catastrophe in the event of severe medical emergency. Meanwhile, any of the rest of us unlucky enough to be caught in some kind of financial whirlpool will have a harder and harder time trying to declare bankruptcy.

Students are working several jobs to go to college. There's nothing wrong with working your way through school. I did it from community college on. But students today often have to stretch classes over more (and more expensive) semesters as they juggle class and workload. Juniors and seniors at the University of Oklahoma, many of whom were middle or upper middle class, told me they were concerned about burdening their parents, financially and emotionally, with their school costs. A number of students, half of whom were young Republicans, were outraged that the Bush administration is cutting some loan programs and freezing others. Such anxiety and frustration is all too familiar, and can be felt at homes and in dorm rooms across the country. The only benefit of Bush's absurd disregard of higher education is if it makes students more aware of the Washington political games that have such an enormous effect on their futures.

Like those students, we know what we need to be secure, but somewhere along the way, we stopped even *asking* for it. What responsibility does our government have to us? Not in empty words but in legislative action? Our government is based on the principle that elected officials should do what we need them to do—first and foremost, they are responsible for us, and accountable to us. Not to giant corporations. Not to lobbyists. Not to Bush's bizarre "conservative" logic that spends what the country doesn't have and leaves Americans to flounder in the wake.

If we look around now, few households can survive without both parents working, and single parents have it much tougher. Yet every corporation is cutting pension benefits and reducing their share of health-care costs. As senior executives in corporate America walk away from botched companies with multimillion-dollar exit packages, in 2005 the Bush conservatives patted themselves on the back for eliminating 140 (mostly) social programs that help middle and lower income Americans—as if that makes them fiscally responsible all of a sudden.[1]

It's time to question what we've let happen. What happened to politicians serving the public? Who are they serving, if not the public? How did we let bad government talk us out of demanding a good one? Why do we idolize the wealthy and allow legislation that undermines our financial opportunity and security? And when did we stop fighting to be a land of equal opportunity?

You've got to ask yourself: what kind of government continually shirks its responsibility to its own citizens in order to save the world, or warns us to better manage our personal budgets when it can't manage the country's? Why not admit that the trillions of dollars in tax cuts are bleeding the United States? And that those tax cuts have put only 600 bucks into the average American's pocket, all of which got eaten up by the amount that health insurance rose in the first six months of 2005.[2] Would you rather have that 600 bucks or guaranteed access to affordable health care? And who exactly is Bush's "ownership society" going to help as the gap between the rich and everyone else continues to grow? We need a new concept of ownership, a vision of political ownership, which is not about investing in the stock market. It's about owning the policies that affect our everyday lives.

Yeah, it's tough out there, but so is cross-country running, and we all did that in elementary school. We need to make it tougher on the people who are making it tougher for us—the ones we elected, the ones sitting in Washington. The "conservatives" who admonish the entire country for not saving enough money, even as their administration runs huge deficits despite cuts to Medicare, Medicaid, higher education, Head Start, and No Child Left Behind. The legislators who bad-mouth Social Security, which has done more to lift real Americans out of poverty than Wall Street ever will.

Let's face it: The Bush government has bungled our domestic priorities. It has overfunded the *wrong* programs, like tax cuts to the top 1 percent of the nation's population; and tax breaks to corporations that profit from war, devastation, and offshore addresses; and war addendums that don't even get included in the budget. Not only is our administration racking up the highest debt and deficit ever, it's asking citizens to start saving money to make up for the fact that it isn't.

Incredibly, Dick Cheney told a crowd of well-dressed pundits and media at a March 2006 Saver Summit that people should stop living paycheck to paycheck.[3] How many of you find that helpful? And exactly what money should we be saving, Dick? Here in the real world, the cost of *everything* we need has risen by more than anything we earn. Save for what? Our own doctors—should we be reduced to comparison shopping for them at Health-Mart? Our retirement—when our wages haven't kept up with inflation, when we get more taken out of our paychecks for health care every month, and when corporate pensions are becoming obsolete? Exactly what money, Dick?

How about instead of fixing Iraq, we do something about fixing Biloxi, Mississippi? Bush says we need to get the job done no matter how long it takes in Iraq. How about we get the same commitment to a national health plan, or affordable higher education for everyone, or a Social Security system that makes us more, not less, secure? How about we roll back some tax cuts and cap some drug prices?

Along the Gulf Coast, I saw people helping each other, families taking in other families, churches giving out food and clothes. I saw people like Darrin Murphy, a jazz and blues musician from New Orleans, who lost *everything* he owned, except for a purple lava lamp and an autographed photo of B. B. King, get up and play the blues for the few people left on Bourbon Street. That man has soul. He's got guts. He lost all his material possessions, but he bought himself a cool bowler hat for his gigs, and he still has spirit. Why can't our government get it? We can face some pretty harsh realities and put ourselves together. Why shouldn't we expect our government to be there with us?

We are this country. It's not about whether we support big or small government. We should all want a government that supports us, that shares our priorities, that is concerned with the physical and economic health of the very people that make this country amazing, and that can manage our money responsibly. We've let the wrong type of government shovel money to its friends and make decisions about our future well-being that we would never make for ourselves.

GET UP IN ARMS

There are simple solutions that can raise the bar for everyone. It's a matter of collectively and repeatedly voicing them, on the Internet, in emails to Congress, in our votes. There are ways our government can make each card in our wallet mean more.

We can raise the salary cap on Social Security to keep the system intact for years to come. We can demand national health care, or at the very least, premium caps on insurance and the right for every individual to be covered. That's what Europeans have and they live longer than we do.[4] (They also get far more paid vacation—almost as much as members of Congress.)

We can demand to know what our money is actually doing in Iraq. We can have the government cap gas prices, rather than offer tax breaks to oil companies already benefiting from the rising cost of getting to work, and taking our kids to school. We can hike the federal minimum wage rate. We can raise federal assistance for college education.

The list is long, but behind it is one basic idea: level the playing field. As Americans, we want similar things and are willing to work for them. We all want healthier wallets. None of us one wants to get jacked by our government.

Get active. It's a midterm election year—a lot of seats are at stake that can push some bad decisions back the other way. And the presidential election will be here before we know it. Be clear about what bugs you most. Think of the items in your wallet, what they mean to you, and what you need them to be. Call or write a letter to your senators and representatives. Write to your local legislators. Google their websites—they all have them. Or, do it the old fashioned way—through snail mail, the U.S. postal service—a public service that we can all use, no matter who we vote for. Tell your friends to mail letters, and your family, and anyone else—it's a 39-cent way to make a statement—the more, the better. Make your voices sit on their office desk.

(And if you really want to make sure you're noticed, don't send that letter directly to the Washington, DC, offices of your congressional representatives; send it to their local offices. Because of a combination of 9/11 and anthrax, everything that goes to the Senate and House is opened and examined. The process takes forever—or at least two months. The letters you mail to that in-state address will be put into a big care package for your congressperson.)

Real politics is about what real people need. We've got to value ourselves enough to push for policies that address our fears, support our needs, and make us and our communities stronger. By digging into the facts, by making our voices heard, by protesting, and by voting, we *can* turn the tide. That's actually an exciting prospect.

Notes

INTRODUCTION

1. Jerry Schwartz, "Voter Turnout Affecting Future of Nation," Associated Press, April 11, 2004.
2. Rukmini Callimachi, "Thousands of Katrina Victims Evicted," *ABC News*, ABC, February 6, 2006, http://www.abcnews.go.com/US/HurricaneKatrina/wireStory?id=1592318&page=1.
3. "Income Picture," *Economic Policy Institute*, August 31, 2005.
4. "Income Picture," *Economic Policy Institute*.
5. "President Signs Energy Policy Act," Office of the Press Secretary, The White House, August 8, 2005.
6. United States Trustee program report for 2004, Department of Justice, http://www.whitehouse.gov/omb/expectmore/summary.10003801.2005.html.
7. "President Signs Bankruptcy Abuse Prevention and Consumer Protection Act," White House Press Release, April 20, 2005.
8. United States Census Bureau Health Insurance Coverage Highlights, 2004.
9. Elise Gould, "Prognosis Worsens for Workers' Healthcare," *Economic Policy Institute*, October 20, 2005.
10. United States General Accounting Office Report, April 2004.
11. "Students to face heavier debt burden," *CNN Money Report*, CNN, February 8, 2006.
12. Jennifer Wheary, "Cuts in College Aid Dim American Dream," *New York Daily News*, June 14, 2005.
13. Sylvia A. Allegretto, "Basic family budgets of working families' incomes often fail to meet living expenses," Economic Policy Institute Briefing Paper, September 1, 2005.
14. Michael A. Fletcher and Richard Morrin, "Bush's Approval Rating Drops to New Low in Wake of Storm," *Washington Post*, September 13, 2005.
15. http://www.wsws.org/articles/2002/nov2002/elec-n07.shtml.
16. Congressional Budget Office figures, 2005, http://www.cbo.gov.

1 YOUR DRIVER'S LICENSE, OIL, AND GAS PRICES

1. "A Primer on Gasoline Prices," Energy Information Administration, Brochure, 2005.
2. Horizontal pipes move oil across land and vertical ones extract it from beneath the ground.
3. "U.S. Senate Approves Bill to Revamp Energy Policy," *Bloomberg*, June 28, 2005, http://www.bloomberg.com.
4. Elisabeth Bumiller, "Bush's Goals on Energy Quickly Find Obstacles," *New York Times*, February 2, 2006.
5. Terrence O'Hara and Amit R. Paley, "Electricity Deregulation: High Cost, Unmet Promises Competition a 'Myth' as Prices Spiral Upward," *Washington Post*, March 12, 2006.
6. "Impacts of the Energy Policy Act 2005," The Senate Committee on Energy and Natural Resources, http://energy.senate.gov/public/_files/ImpactsoftheEnergyBillbrochure.pdf.
7. Ralph Nader, "Bush's Energy Escapades," *Counterpunch*, February 4, 2006.
8. "Greenspan Reassurance Helps Shares Close Mostly Higher," *New York Times*, September 28, 2005.
9. Carl Hulse, "In Raucous House Vote, G.O.P. Oil Refinery Bill Squeaks By," *New York Times*, October 8, 2005.
10. H. Josef Hebert, "Oil Company Executives Defend Profits," Associated Press, November 9, 2005.
11. "Oil Company Executives Defend Profits," Associated Press, November 9, 2005.
12. "Sixteen Percent CEO Turnover at Top Companies in 2005; Cash Separation Payments Range from $0 to $44 Million," BusinessWire, February 7, 2006, http://www.forbes.com.
13. "Citizens for Tax Justice Report," September 2004.
14. Tyson Slocum, "America Needs Oil Company Windfall Profits Tax," *Washington Examiner*, November 24, 2005.
15. Elisabeth Bumiller, "Bush's Goals on Energy Quickly Find Obstacles," *New York Times*, February 2, 2006.

2 YOUR CREDIT CARDS AND OUR NATIONAL DEBT

1. "The Plastic Safety Net: The Reality Behind Debt in America," Demos and the Center for Responsible Lending, October 12, 2005.

2. "The Plastic Safety Net," October 12, 2005.
3. "The Plastic Safety Net," October 12, 2005.
4. Roger Ibbotson, "How U.S. Debt Threatens the Economy," January 5, 2006, http://moneycentral.msn.com/content/invest/extra/P140049.asp.
5. *Bankruptcy Abuse Prevention and Consumer Protection Act of 2005*, 109th Congress.
6. "Senate OKs Bankruptcy Bill 74-25," *CBS News*, CBS, March 11, 2005.
7. Abid Aslam, "Bankruptcy Bill Said to Hit Poorest Americans Hardest," March 12, 2005, http://www.oneworld.net.
8. New York Senator Hillary Clinton abstained, Senate Roll Call, http://www.senate.gov.
9. Figures from the United States Department of Treasury, http://www.treasury.gov.
10. Figures from the United States census put the 2005 population of the United States at 298 million people; http://www.census.gov.
11. Based on 2006 models and prices, http://www.ford.com.
12. Based on data published by the Center for Responsive Politics, http://www.opensecrets.org.
13. http://www.stopatmfees.com.
14. Bankrate.com 2005 annual survey, http://www.bankrate.com/brm/green/chk/basics2-2a.asp.
15. http://www.uspirg.org/reports/atmfeesbacklash2000.pdf.
16. "U.S. Visa Card Usage Hits Record in First Quarter," *San Francisco Business Times*, May 18, 2005.
17. http://www.uspirg.org/reports/atmfeesbacklash2000.pdf.
18. Kathleen Keest, "The Consumer Lending Revolution: Economic Consequences, The Regulatory and Legislative Framework" (presentation, Center for Responsible Lending at St. Louis University School of Law, December 8, 2004).
19. Keest, "The Consumer Lending Revolution," December 8, 2004.
20. "The Effect of Consumer Interest Rate Deregulation on Credit Card Volumes, Charge-Offs, and the Personal Bankruptcy Rate," *FDIC: Bank Trends*, March 1998.
21. "The Plastic Safety Net," October 12, 2005.

3 YOUR EMPLOYEE ID AND THE GONE OLD DAYS

1. http://www.uaw.org/about/uawmembership.html.
2. 2004 Election and Past Election Contribution Data, Center for Responsive Politics, http://www.opensecrets.org/presidential/index.asp.
3. Jonathan Weisman, "President Signs Corporate Tax Legislation; $143 Billion Measure Is Bush's Fifth Major Cut," *Washington Post*, October 23, 2004.
4. http://www.aflcio.org/issues/jobseconomy/jobs/jobcrisis.cfm.
5. Sylvia Allegretto and Jared Bernstein, "The Wage Squeeze and High Health Care Costs," *Economic Policy Institute*, January 27, 2006.
6. "Toyota Closing in on Number One Spot," The Daily Auto Insider, April 11, 2006, http://www.caranddriver.com.
7. Micheline Maynard and Vikas Bajaj, "G.M. to Cut 30,000 Jobs and Close 12 Facilities in 3 Years," *New York Times*, November 21, 2005.
8. "State Senate Passes Bill to Increase Minimum Wage, Schwarzenegger Vetoed Similar Legislation Last Year," *San Francisco Gate*, September 8, 2005.
9. John M. Broder, "States Take Lead in Push to Raise Minimum Wages," *New York Times*, January 2, 2006.
10. Paul Monies, "First of Twelve GM Plants Closes in Oklahoma City," *The Daily Oklahoman*, February 20, 2006.
11. Lee Price, "Economic Snapshots," *Economic Policy Institute*, October 26, 2005.
12. Robert S. McIntyre and T. D. Coo Nguyen, "Corporate Income Taxes in the Bush Years," Citizens for Tax Justice and the Institute on Taxation and Economic Policy, September 2004.
13. Compensation Survey, conducted by the Conference Board and Society of Corporate Secretaries and Governance Professionals, November 8, 2005, http://www.conference-board.org/utilities/pressDetail.cfm?press_ID=2754.
14. "Airline CEO Received Compensation Package Worth Nearly $6 Million," Associated Press, April 11, 2006.
15. "Following the Money in Corporate America," graphic, *New York Times*, November 27, 2005.

4 YOUR STUDENT ID AND EDUCATING AMERICA

1. http://www.studentaidalliance.org.
2. http://www.bankrate.com/brm/definitions.asp?Page=1&channel Id=0&slid=3&termUid=3597.
3. http://www.eschoolnews.com/news/showstory.cfm?ArticleID =6101.
4. MEChA stands for Moviemiento Estudiantil Chicano/a de Aztlan.
5. The League of United Latin American Citizens was established in 1929.
6. "Student Loan Consolidation Rates to Increase; Budget Reconciliation Passes," PRNewswire, February 2, 2006, http://www. prnewswire.com/cgi-bin/stories.pl?ACCT=104&STORY=/ www/story/02-02-2006/0004273096&EDATE=.
7. David Callahan, Tamara Draut and Javier Silva, "Millions to the Middle: Three Strategies to Expand the Middle Class," Demos and the Center for Responsible Lending, August 2004, p. 20.
8. Callahan, Draut and Silva, p. 23.
9. Callahan, Draut and Silva, p. 19.
10. Representative David Obey, "Scrooge-onomics," Appropriations Committee Democrats, December 12, 2005.
11. *Higher Education Act of 1965*, Public Law 89-329, 79 STAT 1219.
12. "Reconciliation Bill Cutting Student Loans Passes by Narrow Margin," http://www.studentaidalliance.org.
13. "Reconciliation Bill Cutting Student Loans Passes by Narrow Margin," http://www.studentaidalliance.org.
14. "Reconciliation Bill Cutting Student Loans Passes by Narrow Margin," http://www.studentaidalliance.org.
15. "News from Congressman George Miller," December 14, 2005, http://www.house.gov/georgemiller.
16. Democratic Policy Committee, "Republicans Cut Important Domestic Programs," Labor-HHS-Education Conference Report, December 15, 2005.

5 YOUR HEALTH INSURANCE CARD AND CARING FOR AMERICA

1. Elise Gould, "Prognosis Worsens for Workers' Healthcare," *Economic Policy Institute*, October 20, 2005.

2. National Coalition on Health Care, http://www.nchc.org/facts/coverage.shtml.
3. House Budget Committee Democratic Caucus, April 28, 2005, http://www.house.gov/budget_democrats/analyses/06instant_analysis_conference_report.pdf.
4. Senate Session, Calendar No. 283, 109th Congress, S. 1969.
5. President Bush's State of the Union address, transcript, January 31, 2006, http://www.whitehouse.gov/stateoftheunion/2006/index.html.
6. http://www.whitehouse.gov/news/releases/2006/02/20060206-2.html.
7. "International Journal of Health Services Study Shows National Health Insurance Could Save $286 Billion on Health Care Paperwork," *Public Citizen/Physicians for a National Health Program*, January 14, 2004.
8. "International Journal of Health Services Study," *Public Citizen*, January 14, 2004.
9. John Leland, "When Health Insurance Is Not a Safeguard," *New York Times*, October 23, 2005.
10. Leland, "When Health Insurance Is Not a Safeguard."
11. Robert Pear, "Drug Plans in Medicare Start Effort in Marketing," *New York Times*, October 1, 2005.
12. "Prescription Drug Prices Under Part D: High and Rising," *CMA Weekly Alert*, February 23, 2006.
13. Joe Conason, *The Raw Deal* (Sausalito, CA: PoliPointPress, 2005), p. 115.
14. "Prescription Drug Prices Under Part D," *CMA Weekly Alert*.
15. Study by Dr. David Himmelstein, associate professor of medicine at Harvard University and co-founder of Physicians for a National Health Program.
16. Deb Reichmann, "Bush Plugs Medicare Prescription D Plan," Associated Press, April 11, 2006.
17. http://money.cnn.com/2006/04/04/news/companies/best investments_f500_fortune.
18. Physicians for a National Health Program is a 14,000-member national group of medical professionals, which advocates for a sustainable health-care plan that covers all Americans.

6 YOUR SOCIAL SECURITY CARD AND KEPING THE FAITH

1. Stephan Richter, "Ben Franklin—The World's First Globalist?" *Boston Globe*, January 19, 2006.
2. 2004 Official Aid and Survivors and Disability Insurance (OASDI) Trustee Report, http://www.ssa.gov/OACT/TR/TR04.
3. Paul Krugman, "Stopping the Bum's Rush," *New York Times*, January 4, 2005.
4. http://www.cbo.gov/showdoc.cfm?index=3214&sequence=0.
5. Paul Krugman, "Gambling with Your Retirement," *New York Times*, February 5, 2006.
6. Carl Malfitano, "Budget Borrows Another $150 Billion of Social Security Surplus," *Region 1 UAW Retiree ALERT*, vol. 7, issue 2, August 2005.
7. Malfitano, "Budget Borrows Another $150 Billion."
8. http://www.cia.gov/cia/publications/factbook/geos/gm.html.
9. 2004 Census Bureau Statistics Data, http://www.census.gov.
10. http://www.seniorjournal.com/NEWS/SocialSecurity/4-12-09 BushVow.htm.
11. Joel Friedman and Aviva Aron-Dine, "Extending Expiring Tax Cuts and AMT Relief Would Cost $3.3 Trillion Through 2016," *Center for Budget and Policy Priorities*, http://www.cbpp.org/2-6-06tax.htm.
12. "Economic Snapshots: Top Earners Get Social Security Windfall, Others Get the Bill," *Economic Policy Institute*, March 9, 2005.
13. Friedman and Aron-Dine, "Extending Expiring Tax Cuts."
14. Allan Sloan, "Bush's Social Security Sleight of Hand," *Washington Post*, February 8, 2006.
15. President Bush's State of the Union address, transcript, January 31, 2006, http://www.whitehouse.gov/stateoftheunion/2006/index.html.

7 YOUR HOME INSURANCE POLICY AND TRUE HOMELAND SECURTY

1. "Senator Lott Introduces Katrina Insurance Measure in Senate," press release. Bill S. 1777, October 27, 2005.

2. Liam Pleven, "Lott Sues Insurer for Storm Damages," *Wall Street Journal*, December 16, 2005, http://www.wsj.com.
3. Pleven, "Lott Sues Insurer for Storm Damages."
4. Drew Jubera, "Post-Katrina Suits Stir up Storm, Legendary Litigator finds Improbable Allies as Complaints Surge along Mississippi Coast," *Atlanta Journal-Constitution*, November 28, 2005.
5. http://www.insurancejournal.com/magazines/southeast/2006/01/02/features/64814.htm.
6. "Insurers Sued for Fraud after Katrina," *CNN Money*, October 5, 2005, http://www.cnnmoney.com.
7. President Bush's State of the Union address, transcript, January 31, 2006, http://www.whitehouse.gov/stateoftheunion/2006/index.html.
8. http://www.wsws.org/articles/2006/mar2006/hall-m01.shtml.
9. Leslie Eaton, "Federal Loans to Homeowners Along Gulf Lag," *New York Times*, December 15, 2005.
10. Congressional Budget Office Projections, February 2006.
11. "Bush Request Would Push War Total to $440 B," Associated Press, February 3, 2006.
12. "President Visits Mississippi Discusses Gulf Coast Reconstruction," St. Stanislaus College, Bay St. Louis, Mississippi, Office of the Press Secretary, Release, January 12, 2006.
13. Shaheen Pasha, "Solid Insurance Outlook in 2006," *CNN Money*, December 30, 2005, http://www.cnnmoney.com.

8 BEYOND YOUR WALLET

1. President Bush's State of the Union address, transcript, January 31, 2006, http://www.whitehouse.gov/stateoftheunion/2006/index.html.
2. National Coalition on Health Care, http://www.nchc.org/facts/coverage.shtml.
3. http://www.whitehouse.gov/news/releases/2006/03/20060302-15.html.
4. http://www.cia.gov/cia/publications/factbook/geos/gm.html.

Acknowledgments

Writing *Jacked* has been an unbelievable experience that simply wouldn't have happened without the love, stories, and support from hundreds of people around the country, including some who have been in my life forever and others who seem as if they have.

A huge thank you to my friends from home: Megan Kiefer, who traveled with me as friend and filmmaker, while we *Thelma and Louise*'d it on the open road. Lauren Rick who cared for my dogs, Sacha and Woody, while I was away. Friends who have been there through my transitions: Margaret Bustell, Vivian Shelton, Deborah Dor, Tracey McCabe, Lynne Roberts, Matt Suroff, Marna Bungers, Robin Lentz, Alex Romero, and Walt Pavlo. Alix Strauss for friendship and writing advice. To Lukas Serafin for being there for me.

I'm thrilled to have worked with the fabulous team at PoliPointPress. Thanks to Peter Richardson, a thorough editor who also guided me through the process of taking *Jacked* from an idea discussed with friends at 2 AM after much wine to what's on these pages. Rhoda Dunn, who never ceases to amaze me with her energy. Also Scott Jordan, Carol Pott, Kim Shannon, Gordon Lee, and Monique Lusse. To David Lobenstine, my meticulous and patient copyeditor, and to the crew at Michael Bass Associates.

I'm grateful to my agent and dear friend, Mark Suroff, who constantly pushes me beyond every limit I set for myself. To my fantastic publicists at Monteiro and Co., particularly Barbara Lombardo, who has shown unwavering commitment.

This country shrank as I realized there are fewer than six degrees of separation between everyone in it. What started as regions on a map and bookings on expedia.com came alive as everyone introduced me to someone who "might be interesting to talk to." In that vein, I owe an extraordinary amount to Gene Carroll at the Cornell Labor Institute, who I'm convinced does know everyone in America. To Mike Schippani at the UAW, Joanne Landy at Physicians for a National Health Program, Dena Shunra, Beth and Rex Yeisley, Scott and Jackie Cooper, Jen Factor, Steve Novick, De Ette Peck, Ozzie La Porte, Adam Payne and Oklahoma University, Jed Wallace, Harry Phillips, and Sonny Brewer.

My gratitude to everyone at Demos, who not only produce amazing research but also are wonderful to work with. Special thanks to Miles Rapoport for his support, as well as to David Callahan, Tammy Draut, Tim Rusch, Donna Parson, and Carol Villano.

Thanks to Colin Robinson for being a consummate cheerleader from the moment I started writing. To everyone who inspired me, through their own work: Ralph Nader, Andy Robinson, John Dizard, Joe Conason, Tracy Quan, Doug Henwood, Michael Perelman, Liza Featherstone, Michael Deibert, Alleen Barber, Joe Nocera, Stan Collender, Max Sawicky, Tom Schlesinger, Randall Dodd, Tyson Slocum, Mike Kissel, Tom Mackell, and Sam Simon.

Thanks to Howard Dean, John Nichols, and Craig Unger for their kind words.

My heartfelt thanks to my family for putting up with my nomadic ways: to my dad and his wife, who pored over every single chapter and word as it went from draft to final form; to my brother and sister-in-law for connecting me to so many people in the state of Texas; and to my sister and brother-in-law for offering warmth and nights out the few times I hit New York City. To my mom, who first suggested I a book questioning the American health-care system.

And to anyone I accidentally left out because of jet lag or sleep deprivation, my sincere apologies and gratitude.

Index

Index

Index

Index

About the Author

Nomi Prins is a journalist and a senior fellow at Demos, a public policy think tank based in New York City. Before becoming a journalist, she served as a managing director for Goldman Sachs in New York and ran the analytics group at Bear Stearns in London.

Her previous book, *Other People's Money: The Corporate Mugging of America*, was chosen as a Best Book of 2004 by *The Economist, Barron's, Library Journal,* and *The Progressive.* Her articles have appeared in the *New York Times, Newsday, Fortune, The Guardian,* and *The Left Business Observer.* Her biweekly column appears in *La Vanguardia,* a Spanish newspaper.

She has appeared as a television commentator on CNBC and the BBC, and she is a frequent guest on Marketplace Radio, Air America, CNN Radio, and many NPR affiliates. She lives in New York City.

OTHER BOOKS FROM
PoliPointPress

Jeff Cohen, *Cable News Confidential: My Misadventures in Corporate Media*
Offers a fast-paced romp through the three major cable news channels—Fox, CNN, and MSNBC—and delivers a serious message about their failure to cover the most urgent issues of the day.
ISBN: 0-9760621-6-X $14.95, soft cover.

The Blue Pages: A Directory of Companies Rated by Their Politics and Practices
Helps consumers make conscious buying decisions using their political and social values.
ISBN: 0-9760621-1-9 $9.95, soft cover.

Steven Hill, *10 Steps to Repair American Democracy*
Identifies the key problems with American democracy and proposes ten specific reforms to reinvigorate it.
ISBN: 0-9760621-5-1 $11.00, soft cover.

Yvonne Latty, *In Conflict: Iraq War Veterans Speak Out on Duty, Loss, and the Fight to Stay Alive*
Features the unheard voices, extraordinary experiences, and personal photographs of a broad mix of Iraq War veterans.
ISBN: 0-9760621-4-3 $24.00, hard cover.

Joe Conason, *The Raw Deal: How the Bush Republicans Plan to Destroy Social Security and the Legacy of the New Deal*
Describes the well-financed and determined effort to undo the Social Security Act and New Deal programs.
ISBN: 0-9760621-2-7 $11.00, soft cover.

John Sperling et al., *The Great Divide: Retro vs. Metro America*
Explains why our nation is so bitterly divided into what the authors call Retro and Metro America.
ISBN: 0-09760621-0-0 $19.95, soft cover.

For more information, please visit www.p3books.com.